THE PALM®
RESTAURANT
COOKBOOK

THE

COOKBOOK

Recipes and Stories from the Classic American Steakhouse

BY BRIGIT LÉGÈRE BINNS

RUNNING PRESS
PHILADELPHIA · LONDON

In memory of Louis "Gigi" Delmaestro
West Hollywood Palm general manager
March 1, 1936 – July 13, 2002

Wonderful father, loving nonno, incredible friend, and extraordinary restaurateur

---

9 8 7 6 5 4 3 2 1
Digit on the right indicates the number of this printing

Library of Congress Control Number: 2002095691

ISBN 0-7624-1583-5

Photography by Jessica Boone
Cover and interior design by Alicia Freile
Edited by Janet Bukovinsky Teacher
Typography: Copperplate and Goudy

This book may be ordered by mail from the publisher.
Please include $2.50 for postage and handling.
But try your bookstore first!

Running Press Book Publishers
125 South Twenty-second Street
Philadelphia, Pennsylvania 19103-4399

Visit us on the web!
www.runningpress.com

— TABLE of CONTENTS —

Chapter Two: Soups and Salads

Chapter Seven: Sides

Chapter Eight: Dishes Made with Leftovers

Chapter Nine: Desserts

A Letter from Bruce Bozzi and Wally Ganzi

None of us would be talking about the Palm today if our fathers, Walter Ganzi Sr. and Bruno Bozzi, had not had the vision to protect the integrity of their restaurant during a time of incredible expansion in the city of New York. If they'd sold out to the skyscraper developers in 1948, we, the proud descendants of two previous generations of Bozzis and Ganzis, would not have had the opportunity to carry on such an extraordinary tradition, and now, to welcome in the fourth generation of Bozzis and Ganzis.

We both started working at the original Palm right out of school, in the early Sixties. Unfortunately, both of our fathers became quite ill at the same time. So we found ourselves in charge, and had the bright idea to expand. At that time, we had twenty-two employees; now we have over 2,000. For a privately owned business to endure, completely intact, through three generations—now, that's amazing. We were the first white-tablecloth restaurant in American to successfully transplant itself to another city. Along the way, not only are there third-generation waiters, but there are third-generation customers, too, like the Millers out in California. All three generations are on the wall at the West Hollywood Palm. Without customers like that, you've got nothing. We both give all of the Palm's customers our heartfelt thanks.

But the guys who helped make the Palm what it has become today are a small core of original "employees." Without them, we couldn't have done even half of this: Tony Tammero, Bruno Molinari, Ray (and soon afterwards, his brother Tommy) Jacomo, Gus Lusardi, Luciano Fiori, Ray Palmer, Gigi del Maestro, Jimmy Martin, Tomas Romano, John Blandino (Johnny B.), and Albino Serpaglia. They couldn't have been any more dedicated if they'd owned the restaurant—in fact, they acted like they owned it—with our blessings, of course. And now, with great confidence, we are passing the company along to Fred Thimm, Bruce's son-in-law, with the incredible team at Palm Management who have brought us to a remarkable 28 restaurants. Fred has now been joined by Bruce Bozzi Jr., a veteran of 37 years in the restaurant business (since the moment he was born).

"No one could ask for a better partner than Wally. In almost forty years of being in business together, we've never had serious argument—and he never allowed any one of his wives to interfere with our relationship."—Bruce Bozzi

"Bruce is my best friend. Nothing and nobody can ever come between us. We have an incredible enduring friendship, fondness, and mutual respect. There's no jealousy, no competition, ever. Over the years a lot of things could have gone wrong, but nothing did because we always stuck together."
—Wally Ganzi

ACKNOWLEDGMENTS

Having come to feel a little like a member of the Palm's extended family, sometimes I have to stop and remind myself that this is a job (albeit one I've been working on for five years). My friend Ellen Hahn (now Ellen Robinson) initiated the first contact. "The Palm wants a cookbook," she said, sometime late in the last century. Ellen has been instrumental in creating this book and in shepherding me through the complex traditions of the Palm family.

This funny, motivated, crazy bunch of people embraced me with no reservations, and over time, I came to understand the strong bond that ties them all together, even in the face of rapid expansion and modern management techniques. For a time, I even considered giving up my precious, but tense, freelance lifestyle to *work* for the Palm.

I attended countless meetings, dinners, and conferences all over the country. I had the unique experience of being the sole nonemployee (and the only woman) at the legendary 75th Anniversary "Old-Guy Dinner" in Washington, D.C., in the summer of 2001. I sat one-on-one with Bruce, and with Wally, and some of the "Old Guys," and heard stories. Oh my, the stories I heard. *Some* of them are in this book.

Now, I wake up in the morning with questions for Tony: Do you want to smash the garlic or chop it? How much cheese goes on the Veal Parmigiana? And then I realize the book is finished, and I'm left feeling a little empty. Then it hits me: almost anywhere I go, there'll always be a Palm.

I'd like to thank:

Ellen, for everything.

Kay, and Coco, in the L.A. Palm kitchen. Thanks for making up all those pesky testing boxes when you had a million other things to do.

Julie Kastrati, Jeff Phillips, and Linda Roth for helping with the quotes, old photographs, motivation, and background.

Fred Thimm, for saying yes to the whole concept, and for his great singing voice.

Jeff Bleaken, for his truly doable desserts and his willingness to drop everything and answer complex questions, and for contributing Chicken New Orleans to my personal repertoire.

Brian McCardle, for lots more answers and his unique, contemporary take on the Palm food.

Sang Ek, for his talented and instinctual hand at combining ingredients, and for his unstoppable enthusiasm (even if it did take six months to get the recipe for Crawfish Etouffe).

Chris Gilman, for excellent laughs along the way and a couple of great stories—again, *some* of them in this book.

Willy Cellucci, Walter McClure, and Michael Cope for the excellent cocktails (in Willy and Walter's case, in a glass as well as on paper).

The Lashers, for persistence and patience!

The late Gigi Delmaestro, for his grudging affection (I know it was never given lightly), and for kind words when things were tough.

Jodi Provost at Horizon Publishing, for help with the cartoons and caricatures for this book.

The lovely Janine Tammero, for putting up with my endless faxed and phoned queries.

Andrea Von Utter, for dropping everything on countless occasions to settle a crucial point.

And to Loren Bosies, Bruce Bozzi Jr., Harriet Sesen, Marc Champagne, Carolyn Graham, Ray and Tommy Jacomo, Jim Longo, Gerard Quinn, the legendary Frankie, and Albino Serpaglia.

Jessica Boone, thank you for capturing the unique food and elegant setting on film with such sensitivity and good humor, and thanks to Susan Draudt, for styling our plates so beautifully while remaining true to the Palm's particular style.

Janet Bukovinsky Teacher, editor extraordinaire, who combines humor, sensitivity, toughness, and a joyful love of food in one very professional package.

For their humor and humility, great big hearts, and for continuing the fine tradition: Wally Ganzi and Bruce Bozzi.

And then there is Tony. Aside from the laughter and a great new vocabulary (ya' big mamaluke!), Tony Tammero taught me more about cooking than I ever imagined was left to learn. For one thing, I'll always cook a perfect steak, and that's no small bananas.

Casey, thanks for smiling through all the veal, and for your smile.

PREFACE

by Larry King

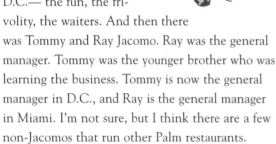

The first time I went to a Palm restaurant was in 1978 when I first moved to Washington, D.C.— the fun, the frivolity, the waiters. And then there was Tommy and Ray Jacomo. Ray was the general manager. Tommy was the younger brother who was learning the business. Tommy is now the general manager in D.C., and Ray is the general manager in Miami. I'm not sure, but I think there are a few non-Jacomos that run other Palm restaurants.

There are three things you can always be sure of when you eat at the Palm:

getting seated quickly
excellent service
and they will never, ever pick up a check.

One of the greatest who-won't-pick-up-the-check stories happened with Tommy Lasorda in D.C. Tommy has never picked up a check in all the time I've known him. It's an art with him. I remember the time I was going to interview him on my radio show. The night before the interview, Tommy took three White House staff people to dinner at the Palm. I stopped by after my show to have coffee with him and the White House guys. The waiter presented the check to Tommy. I think he actually turned colors. He couldn't ask the White House guys to pick up the check, and yet he had an image to uphold. He turned to me and asked, "Aren't I doing your radio show?"

"Yes, you are, Tommy," I said.

"Good, then you pick up this check." And he handed it to me. He's still 0 for 0.

I can safely assure you that whichever dish from this book that you prepare, you will like—no, change that—you will love. Why? Because the Palm prides itself on serving only the best and preparing it in the best way. If you get the best ingredients and follow Tony 's recipes to a "T," you will have a fourth guarantee: the Palm is in your home, so you can pick up your own check!

P.S. If you're smart enough to buy an 837 membership card, carry it at all times. Who knows? You might find yourself in a Palm somewhere in the United States or Mexico, and it'll come in handy.

So now, as my mother used to say, "Sit down, kinder [Yiddish for "children"]— enjoy!"

FOREWORD

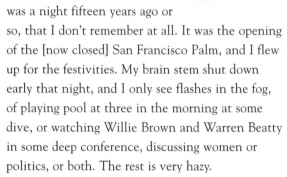

by Brian Dennehy

I guess the most memorable night for me at the Palm, and there were thousands, was a night fifteen years ago or so, that I don't remember at all. It was the opening of the [now closed] San Francisco Palm, and I flew up for the festivities. My brain stem shut down early that night, and I only see flashes in the fog, of playing pool at three in the morning at some dive, or watching Willie Brown and Warren Beatty in some deep conference, discussing women or politics, or both. The rest is very hazy.

Several months later, I slid into a booth at the L.A. Palm and noticed a new photograph hanging on the wall. It was me, sitting in one of the San Francisco Palm booths, a double scotch in one hand and my arm slung around the shoulder of a full-grown chimpanzee, who was gazing at me with boozy affection.

I have no memory of the photo, the chimp, or the rest of the evening, but I will say the chimp never called, never sent flowers, nothing.

I've been enjoying the Palm restaurants for about thirty years now, in one city or another, and I've got the waistline to prove it. In fact, one of the best reasons for going to the Palm, whether you're in Los Angeles, or Atlanta, or Las Vegas, or wherever, is that you'll find the same décor, the same friendly atmosphere, and best of all, the same wonderful food.

Whether you choose a pasta dish, a great salad, or a vegetable plate (if *you're* worried about your waistline), or one of the world-famous steaks, chops, or lobsters, the Palm management has taken great pains to make sure that every Palm restaurant (or "store," as Gigi called them) is providing the highest level of quality, service, and just plain fun.

How do they do it? How do they control the various kitchens so that the New York strip you get in Charlotte is just as good as the one you had last week in Chicago? How do the lobsters, the cottage fries, the onion rings, and the blackened swordfish get that way?

This book will give you some of the answers. Good luck with the recipes, enjoy the food, and then come back to the Palm, any Palm, for the real thing.

Introduction

Where else can former president George H. W. Bush rub shoulders with Senator Ted Kennedy, John Wayne gaze down at a cow that is distinctly *off* the hoof, or Brian Dennehy pilot a sailboat proudly over the head of Sammy Davis Jr.? Where else would Del and Polly Lammers of New York, Peoria, Illinois, and Montgomery, Texas, want to dine together, and bring their children, grandchildren, and cherished friends, for fifty-two years? Where else could two immigrants from northern Italy turn a hole-in-the-wall spaghetti joint into a glamorous yet down-to-earth business that now serves, nationwide, 750,000 steaks and 200,000 lobsters a year at twenty-eight locations in twenty-four cities? Only at the Palm.

The first Palm opened on New York City's Second Avenue in 1926. Through the Great Depression, Prohibition, World War II, the Eisenhower years, and the moon landing, the restaurant thrived and remained virtually unchanged. No matter what else was happening in the world, there were always plenty of loyal customers, and the city's power elite flocked there. The place became so popular that, in 1973, instead of expanding sideways, the owners opened a second restaurant, across Second Avenue, known as Palm Too. In 1976, after *The New York Times* restaurant critic Mimi Sheraton wrote a glowing review of Palm One (the first time that venerable newspaper published a review of a steakhouse), the place became so busy that some nights the management literally had to lock the front door.

Meanwhile, in the early '70s, a great fan of the New York Palms, the elder George Bush, had encouraged Bruce Bozzi and Wally Ganzi, grandsons of the original owners, to expand to Washington, D.C., so he and his friends would

have someplace dependable to eat. Sometimes it seems that the entire Cabinet is in the restaurant, and the political leanings of the staff tend to change, albeit discreetly, with each administration. During the Watergate trial, most of the major players, from Sam Ervin to John Dean, lunched at the Palm every day. But manager Tommy Jacomo (brother of Ray Jacomo, original D.C. manager and now in charge of the Miami Palm) insists the portraits on the wall give equal time to each party.

Around the same time, the writer William Peter Blatty (*The Exorcist*) helped set up financing for the opening of a Palm in Los Angeles. Since business in New York City proved too great for a mere two locations, several years ago the West Side Palm opened at Fiftieth Street between Eighth Avenue and Broadway. Immediately, it was just as packed as the other two. In the intervening years, other Palms have opened in virtually every major city in America, as well as in resort areas of Mexico and Puerto Rico—all places where people like to see and be seen. Now, during the summer, Manhattanites fearing withdrawal can get their steak and lobster fix at the East Hampton Palm, in the lovely old Huntting Inn on Main Street, or at the James Lane Cafe in the Hedges Inn—the latter being technically not a Palm, but another establishment owned by the management.

Perhaps more than any other restaurant in the country, the Palm has gained a reputation as

a major celebrity destination. Yet it resolutely remains a family business, run by the grandsons of the original owners, Pio Bozzi and John Ganzi. (Recently, Pio's great-grandson Bruce Bozzi Jr. became regional director for the Northeast.) Part of the enduring charm is that, while the Palms may be havens for luminaries from the realms of politics, business, entertainment, and sports, they are also special-occasion destinations for regular people, who are treated with as much respect as any past president or current superstar.

At virtually all locations, the clientele is almost ridiculously loyal, and repeat business is extremely high. Consider, for example, Mr. and Mrs. Delmar Lammers of Texas, who first visited the New York Palm in 1950, on a business trip. For the next ten years, on frequent trips to New York, Del unfailingly ate at the Palm. When the Houston Palm opened in 1975, he and Polly celebrated every New Year's Eve, anniversary, and birthday there for the next twenty-three years—despite the fact that it was a 130-mile drive from their home. Now that they've moved closer (only 65 miles away), the Lammers like to lunch at the Palm. "The maitre d' always knows where we like to sit—the third booth from the kitchen. After a bit of conversation, we just tell our favorite waiter, 'the same as usual, Sam—veal piccata for Polly, New York strip for me,' and Sam knows the rest of the meal," says Del.

It's no wonder that once-a-week diners make up 21 percent of the Palm's business; that's 34 percent higher than the national fine-dining average. But those who visit a particular location just once are likely to find it equally compelling. For tourists from abroad, any Palm is an authentic showpiece of American tradition. Business travelers, meanwhile, frequent the reassuringly similar locations across the country (and in San Juan, Cancun, and Mexico City)—each one decorated with cartoons and caricatures of the local "Palmerati."

In terms of food, of course, the Palm is much more than simply the country's finest steakhouse. Regulars know the food is always going to be damn good. In addition to big, prime steaks and even bigger lobsters (three pounds is standard; eighteen-pounders are not unheard of), there is traditional Italian fare, including minestrone, clams oreganato, spaghetti carbonara, veal parmigiana and milanese, and chicken piccata. There are the legendary Palm "name" dishes that regulars tend to order again and again, such as Steak a la Stone, Gigi Salad, and Slater Special. Chefs in each location also create their own up-to-date specials, such as red snapper Capri, honey and pepper-crusted salmon, and sesame-seared ahi tuna with soy vinaigrette.

Though each restaurant is similar—with pressed tin ceilings, dark wood paneling, and leafy green potted palms—there is no feeling of being in a "chain" establishment. Instead, eating there feels like participating in a true American tradition. Each location has a great sense of history,

as does every bite of the Palm's venerable dishes, from Monday Night Salad to the wildly popular creamed spinach.

A LITTLE PALM HISTORY

It was in the 1920s that John Ganzi and Pio Bozzi, recent immigrants from Parma, in Emilia-Romagna, met in New York City. The two men from northern Italy became fast friends, little knowing that they'd be business partners for the rest of their lives and that their descendants three generations on, and more, would be closer than many biological families.

Ganzi and Bozzi decided to start a restaurant together, featuring the food of their hometown. They applied for a business license to open a place called Parma, but the city official misunderstood their Italian-accented English and, instead, they were granted a license to open "Palm." Soon after the restaurant opened, hungry cartoonists from the nearby King Features news syndicate began the tradition of drawing caricatures of regular customers on the walls and ceiling in exchange for dinner. Since the restaurant was frequented by some of New York's most famous and influential citizens, the walls quickly filled up with the best-known faces in the city. Although the partners started out serving Italian food, so many customers asked for steak that John Ganzi often had to run up Second Avenue to the butcher shop. The Palm soon gained a reputation as a place to see and be seen, hammer out a deal, and tuck into a prime steak.

When skyscrapers shot up all around the original Palm in the late '40s, Bozzi and Ganzi declined a lucrative offer to sell out, and the Palm stayed right where it was--and still is. The atmosphere hasn't really changed much since Ganzi used to run out to the butcher shop in 1928. Only the faces have changed. The years seem to fall away when you step into a Palm, whether in Chicago, Las Vegas, Houston, or East Hampton. The familiar caricatures beam down from the walls, while the food is dependably comforting and traditional yet infinitely stylish.

A BUSINESS WITH HEART

The Palm is the oldest continuously operated, family-owned, white-tablecloth restaurant to expand across the country. Today, the Palm Management Group is run by the great grandchildren and great-grandchildren-in-law of John Ganzi and Pio Bozzi.

Their grandsons, Bruce Bozzi and Wally Ganzi, are still involved in decision making at the highest level. They attend every new opening, as do all the existing family members, including, until the mid-1980s, ninety-three-year old Adele Ganzi, widow of John Ganzi. That role is now filled by Gertrude Ganzi, Wally's mother.

Like any company with a long history, the Palm employees consist of the establishment—the "old guys" —and the rookies, known as the "new guys." Actual age has little to do with it—it's more about "making your chops." At the Palm, the lines rarely blur. A new guy might fit in so seamlessly that he almost becomes an honorary old guy, but that doesn't happen often. Sometimes the new guys have bright ideas about efficiency that involve changing the way things are done. The Palm management is not afraid of change—it wouldn't be in business if change hadn't been contemplated, and even put into effect occasionally. In a family-run company with many longtime, surrogate-family employees, change can take time—sometimes a very long time. But when a new idea has been proven effective and (bottom line) profitable, a "new guy" might earn some hard-won respect. At the Palm, profit trickles down, in a very big way. So a good year is more than just a number on a piece of paper—it's college for your kid, or maybe a new car.

The Palm family has become vast in recent years, but there is still a palpable, moving sense of camaraderie. At each semiannual managers' and chefs' meeting, more than a hundred top people are flown to the chosen site and wined, dined, and housed for a few days in the interest of maintaining the sense of fellowship handed down from the first generation of owners. That fellowship is revealed through the funny or emotional stories, the inside and practical jokes that generously pepper the speeches. The other side of this camaraderie is a generous concern. When someone is in trouble, help is there. Whether it's a divorce, money problems, or even a stint in jail, a Palm employee can always go "home" for help— sometimes, quite substantial help.

"I wish the old guys could see this—my dad, Wally's dad. They wouldn't believe what it's become. They were just a couple of guys looking to make a living for their families. Wherever it takes us, I hope we're all together," says Bruce Bozzi, one of the third-generation owners.

TONY ON THE MENU

Throughout this book, you'll hear the unmistakable voice of Tony Tammero, advising and commenting on the recipes. Tony wears the Palm's executive chef's hat, but it's only one hat of many. His sister is married to Bruce Bozzi, which makes him an official member of the inner circle of "Old Italian Guys," as they call themselves, that form the heart of the Palm. Yet he's a chef by nature, the only one in that hallowed group. It is due to Tony's quiet persistence, and his continuing quest for knowledge and skill, that today's Palm food is so tasty and, despite the heft of some of the dishes, so light that regular customers at lunch and dinner are content to eat it five days a week.

Tony started at Palm One on Second Avenue in 1963 and for many years worked a second job at a highly regarded French restaurant to hone his knowledge of fine ingredients and cooking techniques. He didn't make enough money to live by cooking, so he'd go to the dog track a couple of times a week to win enough to support his cooking habit. When Tony started at the Palm, the old chef, Dominic, used to make his spaghetti sauce with ketchup and Tabasco. Tony brought the kitchen out of the dark ages and continues to hand-train every Palm chef, sous-chef, and kitchen worker in the country. Although he travels frequently, today he calls most of the shots, foodwise, from his present post in Miami.

Tony's job is as much diplomat as chef: he has that unique voice capable of bridging the age-old gap between the "front of the house" and "back of the house." He's a top man, a sort of "made guy" in the organization, yet he understands the problems of the kitchen. He stands up for the chefs when the managers threaten to bowl them over. "Remember, guys," he tells the managers. "Your kitchen is the heart of your restaurant. And your prep guys, your dishwashers—they're like the fingers of your hand. You better treat them with respect, or they won't work smooth."

Since virtually all of the original Palm owners and employees came from Parma, they held onto certain expressions from that dialect, like *mamaluco*, which, loosely translated, means "stupid mama's boy." Tony Tammero, however, came from Naples, and that means two things: one, it took a long time for him to prove himself to the guys in the kitchen, and two, he still says *mamaluke*, the Neapolitan dialect version of *mamaluco*.

THE CARICATURES

The first cartoons were painted on the walls in the earliest days of the original Palm as a way for local artists to "sing for their supper" (handy, since the owners had no money for decorating but were willing to part with a plate of spaghetti in exchange for a drawing). Among many others, characters from Mort Walker's *Beetle Bailey*, Matt Weill's *Popeye*, Bill Keane's *Family Circus*, and Chris Brown's *Hagar the Horrible* adorn the walls for posterity. King Features artist Jolly Bill Steinke was an early Palm regular, and he started drawing portraits of other customers as they waited for their dinner. Before long, each wall had become a colorful, living mural. Every new Palm that has opened since features its own combination of "Palmerati": past legends and local luminaries (those who dine regularly at the Palm, that is). In 1995, the original cartoons and caricatures at the New York City Palm were painstakingly restored. For the artwork alone, each of the two dining rooms is insured for half a million dollars.

Mac Miller was the Palm's resident caricaturist for twenty years until his death in 1977, when *Johnny Quest* cartoonist Bill Lignante took over. Bill still does the caricatures for the Los Angeles

Palm. Now, artist Bronwyn Bird, her husband, Bill, and her son Zachary open each new Palm restaurant, drawing and transferring some old portraits and cartoons and creating new faces according to the location. Each face takes anywhere from one to three hours to complete. Many of the subjects have chosen to sign their caricatures—to sign his, Fred Astaire leapt up onto the bar in L.A. and tap-danced across it to inscribe his likeness.

There is nothing quite like the Palm. If this isn't the American dream, then I'm a *mamaluke*. Since the day the first Palm opened in 1926, the motto has been, "Exceed the customer's expectation, and treat everyone who walks through our door as if they are family." After almost five years of working on this book, I know that they mean *everyone*—including the people who walk in through the back door.

Classic
Palm Cocktails

WILLY'S PINKY

"This cocktail was invented during the 1995 Olympic games. Many people believe that the name stems from the fact that, while doing the shooter, I would extend my pinky. However, the truth is that the name is not related to the digit, but rather the color, which is said to resemble the shade of one's eyes after consuming several of them.

"Three ounces of Stoli orange vodka and a splash of cranberry juice are shaken very quickly, so as to chill but not otherwise compromise the vodka, and the drink is strained into a 4-ounce sherry glass. There is lingering debate as to the drink's originator, but frankly, we were all too smashed to remember its exact genesis. I will take full credit, though with the help of Stacy Tompkins and Charlie Bradford." —*Willy Cellucci, Atlanta Palm general manager*

THE FAMOUS MCCLURE COCKTAIL

— MAY BE MADE IN ANY QUANTITY, WITHIN REASON —

This is the invention of Senator John J. McClure (Pennsylvania State Senate, Delaware County, in the 1930s). The recipe was a secret, except to his sons, who were sworn to secrecy until his death in 1965. The senator never had a problem enticing his political friends over to the house, because they anticipated a McClure Cocktail after a session of political strategizing. No matter how many times they asked about the ingredients, he never told, so they kept coming back—exactly as he wanted. The recipe comes to the Palm courtesy of Walter McClure, senior vice president of operations and grandson of its creator. The best quality ingredients make the best cocktail, so feel free to upgrade the brandy to cognac.

2 parts brandy
2 parts gin

1 part orange Curaçao
1 part apricot liqueur

This is not a cocktail where you can "eyeball" the proportions; use a jigger, or a larger measuring device, if appropriate. Prepare the mixture in a pitcher ahead of time, and refrigerate until very, very cold. Not for the weak of heart, this cocktail is not diluted, nor is it garnished. Serve "up" only, in a cocktail glass. It must never, ever touch ice.

THE MICHAEL COPE MARTINI

— YIELD: ONE COCKTAIL —

"I have learned during my twenty-four years with the Palm, in five different cities, that people who drink martinis have very specific requirements. I perfected my method of making a martini in Philadelphia. Most important is to keep the glass filled with shaved ice or, if at home, in the freezer. The colder the better! I use a really large (10-ounce) martini glass at the Denver Palm. Fill a metal mixing cup, or the bottom of a classic cocktail shaker, with ice, and add about 6 ounces of your favorite vodka or gin. Use the bar spoon to pulverize the ice. Don't just stir it. Get an attitude!! Take your glass out of the freezer, put 2 olives on a toothpick (make sure the olives are dripping with olive juice), and place it in the glass. Strain the vodka or gin from the shaker cup into the chilled glass. If ice crystals form on the surface, you can't go wrong!

I am a purist, and I have my own opinions about all the "designer martinis": if you don't like the taste of the booze, then don't drink it. Don't add juices and sweeteners to martinis. You destroy the myth." —*Michael Cope, Denver Palm bartender*

During one of New York City's more recent, famous blizzards, Palm co-owner Bruce Bozzi ended up tending bar because most of the staff couldn't make it into the city. As seems to happen whenever there is a crisis, the Palm was jam-packed (when times get tough, it's good to be with one's fellow man—and a cocktail). Bruce hadn't tended bar in years, but he was staying above water, barely. When a customer ordered a Tom Collins, however, Bruce's reply was, "What's your second choice?"

JEFF PHILLIPS' HOT BLUEBERRY TEA

"You take a snifter and add 1 ounce of Grand Marnier. Then add ½ ounce of blackberry brandy. The combination of the orange liqueur and the blackberry give it the blueberry flavor. Then you fill the snifter with hot water and squeeze in a whole wedge of lemon. Stir and enjoy. It will not cure your cold, but it will help you sleep." —*Jeff Phillips, vice president of marketing*

— CHAPTER 1 —

Appetizers

CLAMS CASINO

— SERVES 4 —

Like oysters and mussels, clams should be alive until they're shucked and cooked. When you handle them prior to shucking, any open clam that does not close should be discarded. To shuck live clams, use a sturdy paring knife or oyster knife, and wear a protective glove or place a wadded-up tea towel in the hand holding the clam. Insert the tip of the knife carefully opposite the hinge and, once it is in, be sure to move it along the top shell so you don't cut the clam in half. Once the clam is open, use the knife to release the meat from the bottom shell. If desired, unshucked clams may be refrigerated in a large bowl, covered with a damp cloth, for up to two days before cooking.

¾ pound unsalted butter, cut into 16 pieces,
    at cool room temperature
2 large cloves garlic, chopped
¼ cup loosely packed flat-leaf parsley leaves
¼ cup drained pimento, coarsely chopped
1 rib celery, finely diced

¼ pound thinly sliced bacon, cut into 24
    (1-inch) squares
24 small clams, preferably from eastern waters,
    shucked and still on their bottom shells
1 cup clam juice
¼ cup dry white wine

In a food processor, combine the butter, garlic, parsley, and pimento. Process until evenly combined, transfer to a bowl, and fold in the celery. Scoop up about 1 tablespoon of the prepared butter, and mold it smoothly over the top of each shucked clam on the half shell. Place the prepared clams on a tray. If desired, cover and refrigerate for up to 4 hours.

In a saucepan of rapidly boiling water, blanch the bacon for 5 minutes. Drain on paper towels and pat dry. Press a square of bacon onto the top of each butter-topped clam.

Preheat a broiler to high heat. In an ovenproof sauté pan that will fit under your broiler, arrange the clams butter-side up (cook in two batches, if necessary). Drizzle the clam juice and wine around the edge of the pan. Place under the broiler, about 4 inches from the heat source, until the butter has melted, the clams are firm, and the bacon has crisped slightly, about 2 minutes. Transfer the finished clams to serving plates, being careful not to spill out too much of the juice; keep warm while you finish broiling the remaining clams and transfer them to serving plates.

Over high heat, boil the pan juices very rapidly for about 1 minute, shaking the pan vigorously to bring the juices together into a thin sauce. Drizzle a little sauce over the clams and serve at once.

"Edward Bennett Williams, the famous trial lawyer, came into the Palm with Joe DiMaggio. As they walked to the table, the entire restaurant spontaneously stood up and gave them a standing ovation. It would have brought a tear to a brass eye."

—Tommy Jacomo, former Washington, D.C., manager

CLAMS OREGANATO

— SERVES 3 PALM-STYLE, OR 4 —

"This is a classic appetizer. Nothing goes together better than Italian breadcrumbs, garlic, good Parmesan cheese, and oregano. This mixture can be used as a filler or a topper. The key is to use the freshest clams possible and open them just before you're ready to prepare the dish." —Brian McCardle, Palm One chef

¾ cup dry Italian breadcrumbs
2 cloves garlic, minced
2 tablespoons pure olive oil
¼ cup grated Parmigiano-Reggiano
1½ teaspoons dried oregano
2 tablespoons finely chopped flat-leaf parsley
3½ tablespoons dry white wine

24 small clams, preferably from eastern waters, shucked and still on their bottom shells (see clam-shucking instructions on page 30)
½ cup clarified butter
¾ cup clam juice
¼ cup chicken stock or water
1 tablespoon unsalted butter, at room temperature

In a mixing bowl, combine the breadcrumbs, garlic, olive oil, Parmigiano, oregano, parsley, and 1½ tablespoons white wine. Mix with a fork to blend thoroughly. The mixture should be quite damp, almost wet. Scoop up about 1 tablespoon of the breadcrumb mixture, and use the palm of your hand to mold it firmly over the top of each clam. If desired, at this point the clams may be covered and refrigerated for up to 24 hours.

Preheat a broiler to high heat. In an ovenproof sauté pan that will fit under your broiler, arrange the clams breadcrumb-side up (cook in two batches, if necessary). Drizzle a touch of clarified butter evenly over each clam; then drizzle the clam juice, stock, and remaining 2 tablespoons of wine around the edge of the pan. Place under the broiler, about 4 inches from the heat source, until the topping is crisp and golden, 3 to 4 minutes. Transfer the finished clams to serving plates. Keep warm while you finish broiling the remaining clams, if necessary, and transfer them to serving plates.

Over high heat, boil the pan juices very rapidly for about 1 minute, shaking the pan vigorously to bring the juices together into a thin sauce. Swirl in the unsalted butter, and keep shaking the pan until the butter is blended in. Drizzle a little sauce around the edge of each plate and serve at once.

Clarified butter is used whenever the taste of butter is desired but the high cooking temperature would cause whole butter to burn. To make it, melt ½ pound butter (any less is difficult to work with) over very low heat in a small, heavy-bottomed saucepan. Do not disturb the butter as it slowly melts. Turn off the heat. Spoon off and discard the pale white foam that has risen to the top. Very gently, pour the clear butter into a glass jar, leaving behind the milky white residue that has settled to the bottom of the pan. Cover the jar and refrigerate the clarified butter until needed. It will keep almost indefinitely.

CLAMS BIANCO

— SERVES 2 —

This recipe can easily be doubled by using two large sauté pans; the clams do not enjoy being crowded. Leaving the garlic in with the clams makes for a rustic presentation and a super-garlicky flavor.

2 tablespoons pure olive oil
16 small clams, preferably from eastern waters,
    scrubbed clean
2 large cloves garlic, crushed with the side
    of a large, heavy knife
3 leaves fresh basil
⅓ cup dry white wine

⅓ cup chicken stock
⅛ teaspoon red pepper flakes
1 tablespoon unsalted butter,
    at room temperature
Fine sea salt
Crusty bread, for dipping

Place a 12-inch sauté pan over high heat and add the oil. When the oil is hot, gently place the clams in the pan and add the garlic, whole basil leaves, and wine. Cover the pan and cook for 6 to 10 minutes, until the clams have opened (discard any clams that have not opened after 10 minutes; however, really large clams may take up to 20 minutes to open). Do not shake the pan. Uncover, add the stock, and let it reduce slightly, for about 3 minutes.

Add the red pepper and the butter, and shake the pan back and forth to emulsify the butter into the sauce. Remove from the heat and taste for seasoning; clams are briny, so the sauce may not need additional salt. Spoon the clams and sauce, including the crushed garlic and basil, into two heated bowls and serve at once with crusty bread.

SLATER SPECIAL

— SERVES 4 —

"I took the very best the Palm had to offer and made it into an appetizer-size special, which I only served to my good customers. But then, of course, everyone liked it, so we just started serving this at lunch and dinner, in Vegas, in L.A, and before you knew it, all over the company." — Dick Slater, nineteen-year veteran server at Las Vegas Palm

"A Slater Special is just one crab cake and one Shrimp Bruno, but I like to use less sauce than on the Bruno, because otherwise it will soak into the crab cake and make it soggy." —Tony Tammero, executive chef

4 cooked Crab Cakes (page 72), kept warm
½ cup all-purpose flour, for dredging
1 large egg, well beaten
2 tablespoons canola oil
4 jumbo (U-12) shrimp, shelled, deveined, and butterflied, with tails left on (see Note)
1 small clove garlic, crushed with the side of a large, heavy knife

¼ cup dry white wine
1 tablespoon fresh lemon juice
⅛ teaspoon fine sea salt, or to taste
1 teaspoon Dijon mustard
1 tablespoon unsalted butter, at room temperature
½ teaspoon very finely chopped flat-leaf parsley
4 lemon wedges, for serving

Place each of the finished crab cakes on a serving plate, and keep them warm in a low oven while you make the Shrimp Bruno.

Place the flour and the beaten egg in two separate shallow bowls near the stove. In a medium sauté pan, heat the oil over medium-high heat. Dredge the shrimp in the flour, shaking off the excess. Dip each shrimp into the egg wash, letting the excess drip back into the bowl for a moment. Add the crushed garlic to the pan; then place the shrimp, butterflied side down, in the hot oil. Cook undisturbed for 4 minutes, until pale golden. (Cook the shrimp in batches, if necessary, to avoid overcrowding).

Drain off all but about 1 teaspoon of the cooking oil. Add the white wine, lemon juice, and salt. Bring to a boil, and cook for 1 minute. Transfer each shrimp to one of the heated plates, alongside a crab cake. Increase the heat to high. Whisk in the mustard and simmer the sauce until it is reduced by two-thirds, about 1 minute. Remove the pan from the heat and swirl in the butter, shaking the pan vigorously to bring the sauce together. Discard the garlic and spoon a little sauce over each shrimp. Sprinkle the edges of the plates with a little parsley, place a lemon wedge on the side, and serve at once.

Note: To butterfly shrimp, run a sharp knife along the back, rounded edge of the peeled shrimp, cutting about three-quarters of the way—but not all the way through to the other side. Open the shrimp out to the sides like a book.

The Real Slater Special

"When I was GM at the Las Vegas Palm, I ran a sales contest to see which waiter could sell the most appetizers. The prize was a ticket to L.A. and dinner at the L.A. Palm. We ran the numbers every day, and a waiter named Dick Slater was ahead of everybody else. When I asked him how he did it, he said he encouraged each table to get platters of appetizers and pass them around family-style. But people liked the combo so much that they wanted to order it individually, so we ended up putting the Slater Special on the menu. Slater never collected his prize. While he was driving from Memphis to Texas, he got stopped in West Monroe, Louisiana, while transporting 105 pounds of an illegal substance sometimes smoked by unscrupulous people. He had to take a three-year vacation. We sent him letters, magazines, and cigarettes, and told the authorities he still had a job, so they let him out a little early, and he came back to the Las Vegas Palm. He's still there. And he's still a great salesman. But I don't think we ever gave him his trip to the L.A. Palm." —*Walter McClure, senior vice president of operations*

SHRIMP BRUNO

— SERVES 4 —

This dish was named after a waiter in Los Angeles. It should not be confused with Chicken Bruno, named after Bruno Bozzi, son of the original owner of the Palm and father of Bruce Bozzi, the current co-owner.

½ *cup all-purpose flour, for dredging*
3 *large eggs, well beaten*
½ *cup canola oil*
12 *jumbo (U-12) shrimp, shelled, deveined, and butterflied, with tails left on (see Note on page 34)*
2 *large cloves garlic, crushed with the side of a large, heavy knife*

¾ *cup dry white wine*
3 *tablespoons fresh lemon juice*
¼ *teaspoon fine sea salt, or to taste*
1 *tablespoon Dijon mustard*
3 *tablespoons unsalted butter, at room temperature*
2 *teaspoons very finely chopped flat-leaf parsley*
4 *lemon wedges, for serving*

Warm 4 serving plates in a low oven. Place the flour and the beaten eggs in two separate shallow bowls near the stove. In a 12-inch sauté pan, heat the oil over medium-high heat. Dredge the shrimp in the flour, shaking off the excess. Dip each shrimp into the egg wash, letting the excess drip back into the bowl for a moment. Place the shrimp, butterflied side down, in the hot oil. Cook undisturbed for 3 minutes, until pale golden. Add the garlic and cook for 1 minute more, stirring. (Cook the shrimp in batches, if necessary, to avoid overcrowding).

Drain off all but about 1 teaspoon of the cooking oil. Add the white wine, lemon juice, and salt. Bring to a boil and cook for 1 minute. Transfer the shrimp to heated plates and increase the heat to high. Whisk in the mustard and simmer the sauce until it is reduced by two-thirds, about 2 minutes. Remove the pan from the heat and swirl in the butter, shaking the pan vigorously to bring the sauce together. Discard the garlic and spoon a little sauce over each serving. Sprinkle the edges of the plates with parsley, place a lemon wedge on the side, and serve at once.

> ## "I wouldn't call the Palm my restaurant. I'd call it my second home."
>
> —James Carville

GRILLED JUMBO SHRIMP OVER BABY FIELD GREENS

— SERVES 6 —

This is a great outdoor dish for spring or summer. Everything can be prepped ahead of time: the vinaigrette mixed, the shrimp marinating, the salad assembled. Then you just throw the shrimp on the grill and toss the salad at the last minute. Slow-roasting the garlic and peppers creates a rich, complex flavor.

2 red bell peppers, halved, cored, and seeded

2 cloves garlic, crushed with the side
of a large, heavy knife

2 tablespoons olive or canola oil

Fine sea salt and freshly ground black pepper

$\frac{1}{3}$ cup red wine vinegar

1 tablespoon balsamic vinegar

1 teaspoon sugar

$\frac{1}{2}$ teaspoon Cajun spice blend or chile powder

$\frac{1}{4}$ cup loosely packed basil leaves

$\frac{1}{2}$ cup extra-virgin olive oil

2 pounds jumbo shrimp (U-12), shelled,
deveined, and butterflied, with tails left on
(see Note on page 34)

$\frac{1}{2}$ pound mixed baby field greens (mizuna,
lamb's lettuce, frisée, radicchio, etc.),
washed and thoroughly dried

Preheat the oven to 250°. In a small roasting pan, toss the peppers with the crushed garlic and olive or canola oil. Season with salt and pepper, and roast for about 2 hours, until blistered and completely tender. In a blender, combine the roasted peppers and garlic, the two vinegars, sugar, Cajun spice blend, and basil. Blend to a puree; then add the extra-virgin olive oil and blend again until smooth. Taste for seasoning. In a large bowl, combine half the red pepper vinaigrette with the shrimp and toss to coat evenly. Cover and marinate in the refrigerator for at least 4 hours, preferably overnight.

Prepare a charcoal or gas grill for medium-high heat grilling, or heat a cast iron stovetop griddle. Remove the shrimp from the marinade with a slotted spoon, and grill for about 1$\frac{1}{2}$ minutes on each side, until charred, pink, and firm.

Toss the field greens with enough of the remaining red pepper vinaigrette to lightly coat all the leaves. Mound onto six plates, place a few shrimp on top, and serve at once.

"I became the manager at Palm One when Wally [Ganzi] went out to L.A. to open a Palm there. The first time we ever had a written menu there was 1993. I was the manager until 1995, and when I retired, there were three or four waiters who had been at the Palm for thirty-eight, forty years. We were all about the same age, and we all retired together. We always had sawdust on the floor, too, right up until the mid-90s—in all the Palms. Every day at lunch, and then again at dinner, we had to sweep it all up and replace it."

—Bruno Molinari

CALAMARI FRITTI

— SERVES 4 —

Squid is one seafood that does not suffer from being frozen, and if you can find cleaned frozen squid, so much the better. If the cephalopods have not been cleaned, it's quite simple to find the "beak" and pull it out of each tube-shaped body. It looks like a piece of opaque plastic, pointed at one end and about the length of the tube itself. Pull the hard cartilage out of the tentacles, and you're in business.

12 ounces fresh or frozen (thawed) calamari, bodies cut into ½-inch rings and tentacles left intact
1 cup milk
Fine sea salt and freshly ground black pepper
About 2 quarts vegetable or canola oil, for deep frying

1½ cups all-purpose flour, for dredging
½ cup fine yellow cornmeal, for dredging
½ small head iceberg lettuce, cut into julienne
1 lemon, cut into 4 wedges, for garnish
1½ cups Marinara Sauce (page 146), or best-quality bottled marinara sauce
1 tablespoon finely chopped flat-leaf parsley

Soak the calamari in the milk with a pinch of salt and pepper, covered and refrigerated, for at least 1 hour and up to 4 hours. Drain in a colander.

Preheat the oven to 250°. In a wide 8- or 10-quart stockpot or a deep fryer, heat about 3 inches of oil over high heat to 375° on a candy or deep-frying thermometer. Do not fill the pan more than half full with oil. Place it at the back of the stove if possible, for safety. In any event, you must use your most powerful burner.

In a large, shallow bowl, combine the flour and cornmeal and season generously with salt and pepper. When the oil reaches the desired temperature, add half the drained calamari to the flour mixture and toss with your hands to coat each piece evenly. Return to the colander and shake to remove any excess dredging mixture. Place the calamari rings in a large skimmer or a fryer basket and lower carefully into the hot oil. Fry, nudging occasionally to help them brown evenly, until the rings are crispy and golden brown, about 1 minute. Remove with the skimmer, letting the oil drain for a few seconds, and place on a baking sheet lined with paper towels. Keep the first batch warm in a low oven while you wait for the oil to return to 375°. Do not attempt to fry the second batch of calamari until the oil reaches the correct temperature, or you will be left with a soggy, oily mess. Fry the second batch the same way.

Mound an equal amount of the julienned lettuce on each of four plates, and place a lemon wedge and a ramekin of Marinara Sauce on the side of the plate. Top the lettuce with fried calamari and a little chopped parsley, and serve at once.

SESAME-SEARED AHI TUNA WITH FIELD GREENS AND SOY VINAIGRETTE

— SERVES 6 —

"Sang Ek, head chef at the Palm in Washington, D.C., was the first Palm chef to cook with Asian ingredients, but for a long time he only used them in lunch specials in D.C. This dish was born at the West Side Palm in New York City, when we first opened. Then it became so popular that we took it countrywide — the first dish with Asian ingredients to make it onto the core menu. This is actually my dish, but I'll bet Sang will take credit for it if you give him a chance." —Tony Tammero, executive chef

SOY VINAIGRETTE:

½ cup plum sauce
½ cup hoisin sauce
3 tablespoons light sesame oil
1½ tablespoons pineapple juice
1½ tablespoons soy sauce

1 teaspoon minced orange zest
1 teaspoon grated or very finely chopped
*   fresh ginger*
1 small clove garlic, very finely chopped

TUNA:

1 cup light sesame oil

1 cup soy sauce

1 cup water

1 tablespoon grated fresh ginger

1 small clove garlic, very finely chopped

½ teaspoon freshly ground black pepper

1½ pounds center-cut, sushi-grade ahi tuna, cut into 6 pieces

¼ cup white sesame seeds, toasted in a dry pan until golden (plus extra for garnish)

1 tablespoon olive oil

1¼ pounds mixed baby field greens (mizuna, lamb's lettuce, frisée, radicchio, etc.; about 6 cups loosely packed), washed and thoroughly dried

1 red bell pepper, cored, seeded, and cut into fine julienne

1 yellow bell pepper, cored, seeded, and cut into fine julienne

2 tablespoons white sesame seeds, toasted in a dry pan until golden, for garnish

Deep-fried wonton wrappers, for garnish (optional)

In a mixing bowl, whisk together the plum sauce, hoisin sauce, sesame oil, pineapple juice, soy sauce, orange zest, ginger, and garlic. Set aside until serving time.

In a shallow baking dish, combine the sesame oil, soy sauce, water, ginger, garlic, and black pepper. Add the tuna pieces, turn to coat both sides, and let marinate for 30 minutes, turning again halfway through the marinating time. Drain the tuna, discarding the marinade, and pat dry with paper towels. Place the toasted sesame seeds on a large plate, and coat both sides of each tuna piece with the seeds, pressing down gently to help them adhere.

Place a large nonstick skillet over medium-high heat, and add the olive oil. Add the tuna (cook in two batches to avoid overcrowding the pan, if necessary). Sear the tuna for 1 minute on each side for medium-rare, 2 minutes longer if you prefer it cooked through to the center. Transfer the seared tuna to a platter, and let cool to room temperature; then chill for at least 30 minutes.

In a large mixing bowl, toss the field greens and the pepper julienne with just enough of the soy vinaigrette to coat the leaves; reserve the remaining vinaigrette for another use. Mound an equal quantity of greens on each of 6 plates. Quickly cut each piece of tuna into 5 or 6 slices, about ¼ inch thick. Fan the tuna slices around the salad, and scatter the sesame seeds and the fried wonton wrappers (if using), over the top. Serve at once.

BEEF TARTARE

— SERVES 4 —

Everyone has heard the old story about the wag-about-town who went to the "21" Club and ordered steak tartare. When it arrived, he told the waiter to take it back to the kitchen and cook it medium-rare. That, he felt, was the only way to get a really superb hamburger. This classic is not for the faint of heart, but if you love a sweet, pink tartare, this will be your new favorite recipe. Remember that cold mixtures require a more generous hand with seasoning, since tastebuds have a harder time distinguishing flavors when food is cold. So don't stint on the salt and pepper.

1 French baguette, sliced ¼-inch thick
1 pound best-quality beef filet, placed in
   the freezer for 30 minutes to firm
3 to 4 ounces very finely chopped white onion
   (about half a medium onion)
2 tablespoons capers, rinsed, drained,
   and finely chopped

2 teaspoons Worcestershire sauce
Fine sea salt and freshly ground black pepper
1 hard-boiled egg, peeled and finely chopped
1 tablespoon finely chopped flat-leaf parsley,
   for garnish

Preheat the oven to 350°. Chill a medium mixing bowl and 4 small plates in the refrigerator. Spread the baguette slices on a baking sheet, and toast in the oven for 15 minutes, until crisp and slightly golden.

With a very sharp knife, slice the beef thinly across the grain; then cut each slice into ¼-inch strips. Turn the strips at a right angle to the knife, and slice them again, crosswise, at ⅛-inch intervals. In the chilled bowl, combine the diced beef with the onion, capers, Worcestershire sauce, 1 teaspoon salt, and ¼ teaspoon pepper. Add the hard-boiled egg, and toss quickly but thoroughly with 2 forks to combine. Taste and correct seasoning, if necessary. Do not overwork the mixture.

Using your (clean) hands, quickly form the tartare mixture into 4 hamburger-shaped patties and place one on each of the chilled plates. Arrange toasted baguette slices around the rim of the plate, scatter with the parsley, and serve at once.

HEARTS OF PALM SALAD

— SERVES 4 —

Carlo Bruno used to be the executive chef at the Houston Palm, and he came up with this recipe because he thought the Palm needed a dish using hearts of palm. For a while, it was only available in Houston, but now it's on menus around the country. Hearts of palm vary in tenderness and quality. They can be woody and mushy—sometimes in the same can! Spanish hearts of palm are always good.

12 pale inner leaves from the heart of
  a romaine lettuce
1¼ pound best-quality canned hearts of palm
  (preferably from Spain), drained and
  halved lengthwise
2 medium ripe tomatoes, cored and cut into
  ¼-inch dice
24 kalamata olives

4 hard-boiled eggs, peeled and cut into quarters
Basic Vinaigrette (page 65) with julienned
  fresh basil, Blue Cheese Dressing (page 64),
  Jeffrey's Famous Dressing (page 67),
  Balsamic Dressing (page 68), or Roasted
  Red Pepper Dressing (page 67), for serving

Cut the romaine leaves crosswise into thin strips. On 4 chilled salad plates, make a bed of lettuce and arrange the hearts of palm in parallel rows on top. Place a line of diced tomato at a crosswise angle, running from left to right on top of the hearts of palm. Place 6 olives in a pile at the bottom of the plate, and distribute the hard-boiled egg quarters at the top. Serve with the dressing of your choice on the side.

The opening party for a new Palm is a momentous, often riotous event. These days, the parties have been coming thick and fast, but no one ever takes success for granted. From all over the country, everyone in Palm senior and middle management, and everyone who is anyone in the city itself, is there. My first Palm opening was in San Antonio, Texas. Wally Ganzi introduced the mayor, who noted that there were two previous San Antonio mayors also in attendance. The Palm was a part of the city's Houston Street revitalization project, virtually the flagship for an exciting process in a lovely and very historic city. After the big rush of attendees thinned out, the remaining Palm family was serenaded by a salsa band. It was like a big wedding, where everyone in the family still gets along.

Asparagus Fritti

Adding a little butter to the frying oil helps the crust to brown faster and adds a rich flavor that nicely complements the "King of Vegetables."

1¼ pounds medium asparagus
1 cup all-purpose flour, for dredging
2 large eggs, well beaten
1 cup seasoned dry Italian breadcrumbs
   or panko (Japanese breadcrumbs),
   generously seasoned with salt and pepper

1 cup canola oil
1 tablespoon unsalted butter,
   at room temperature
1 lemon, cut into 4 wedges, for serving

Snap off the woody ends of the asparagus stems and, if desired, peel about 2 inches of the base of each spear to help them cook more evenly. Bring a wide pan of lightly salted water to a rolling boil, and blanch the asparagus for 1 minute. Drain and spread the spears on paper towels to dry for 5 to 10 minutes.

Place three shallow bowls near the stove, and place the flour in one, the beaten eggs in the second, and the seasoned breadcrumbs in the third. Roll the asparagus first in the flour, then slide them into the egg wash, letting the excess drain away for a moment, and finally, turn in the breadcrumbs, shaking off any excess.

Place a 12-inch sauté pan over medium-high heat, and add the oil. When the oil is hot but not smoking, add the butter. Add some asparagus to the pan, without overcrowding. Fry the first batch of asparagus, turning occasionally with tongs, until golden, about 4 minutes. Carefully transfer the fried spears to paper towels to blot off the excess oil, and keep warm in a low oven while you fry the remaining asparagus. Transfer to warmed serving plates and serve at once, with the lemon wedges on the side.

Mimi Sheraton wrote in *The New York Times* in 1976, "The reason for Palm's [sic] enduring success, often when other places around town are deserted, is that it is an original. It is not a result of clever merchandising gimmicks created by high-priced consultants, and the Bozzis and Ganzis do not look over their shoulders to see what other restaurateurs are up to. Dishes here are not compared to Italian originals; their authenticity is beyond question. All are heartily, gloriously, authentically Palm-style."

— CHAPTER 2 —

Soups and Salads

LOBSTER BISQUE

— SERVES 6 TO 8 —

"Sang is responsible for this bisque, and it's great. I like the way he uses rice for a thickener." —Tony Tammero, executive chef

If fish stock is not available, use chicken broth or stock rather than bottled clam juice to make the lobster stock.

LOBSTER STOCK:

2 live 1½-pound lobsters
2 tablespoons unsalted butter
1 medium yellow onion, coarsely chopped
½ cup sliced carrots
½ cup sliced celery

3 sprigs fresh thyme
10 black peppercorns
1 cup dry white wine
8 cups homemade fish stock

LOBSTER BISQUE:

1 tablespoon unsalted butter
½ medium yellow onion, coarsely chopped
¼ cup sliced carrots
¼ cup sliced celery
1 teaspoon best-quality curry powder
⅛ teaspoon cayenne pepper

1 cup brandy
About 8 cups Lobster Stock
⅓ cup arborio rice
⅓ cup tomato paste
1 cup heavy cream
Fine sea salt and white pepper

For the Lobster Stock: Cut each lobster in half, lengthwise, through the belly. Remove and discard the stomachs and intestines, chop the claws in half, and chop each of the bodies into 4 pieces. Place a large pot over medium heat, and add the butter. Toss in the lobster pieces and sauté, stirring and crushing the shells a little with a meat mallet or other heavy implement, until the shells are red, about 8 minutes. Add the onion, carrots, celery, and thyme, and sauté, stirring, until the vegetables are tender, about 10 minutes. Add the peppercorns and the wine, and simmer until reduced by about half. Add the fish stock, and adjust the heat so that the liquid is simmering gently. Simmer, uncovered, stirring occasionally, for 30 minutes. Strain through a colander into a large bowl, pressing down on the solids to extract as much flavor as possible. If any meat is left in the lobster shells, you can pull it out and reserve it for serving time, but most of the meat and flavor will now be in the stock. Discard the remaining solids, and reserve all the stock for use in the bisque. (The stock may be made ahead of time, then cooled, covered, and refrigerated for up to 1 day.)

For the Lobster Bisque: In a large, clean pot, melt the butter over medium-low heat. Add the onion, carrots, and celery, and sweat gently until translucent, about 6 minutes. Stir in the curry powder and the cayenne, and cook for 1 minute more. Add the brandy, and increase the heat to medium-high. Simmer until reduced and slightly syrupy, about 5 minutes. Add the reserved Lobster Stock, rice, and tomato paste. Stir to blend, and adjust the heat so that the soup simmers gently for 30 minutes, until the rice is very tender. Use an immersion blender to puree the soup until smooth. Over low heat, stir in the cream and heat through, but do not allow to boil. Press the soup through a fine sieve, and return to a clean saucepan. Add salt and white pepper to taste, and serve in shallow bowls, garnished with any reserved lobster meat.

"Just after we opened the D.C. Palm, I used to take the Amex slips up to New York by shuttle because I couldn't wait 5 to 7 days for the credit card company to pay up. I had to pay the purveyors, and the cash flow just couldn't take it. So I'd fly up, drop the slips at the bank, have lunch at the Palm, pick up the cash, take the shuttle back to D.C. and pay the vendors the next day. We had no idea what we were doing. Bush [former President George H. Bush] wanted someplace to eat after he moved to D.C., so we opened a Palm. You could say we learned as we went along. "

—*Ray Jacomo, original manager of the Washington, D.C., Palm, now manager at the Miami Palm*

STRACIATELLA ROMANO

— SERVES 6 TO 8 —

"This is a very old-fashioned soup. I think Dominic came up with it back in the Sixties. He used to build these fantastic churches out of matchsticks. I don't mean two-hits-and-a-miss, either—these were major constructions. People used to come from all over the neighborhood, up above Palm One, to see these miracles Dominic put together out of matchsticks and glue." —Tony Tammero, executive chef

1 head escarole
5 large eggs
1 teaspoon fine sea salt, or to taste
½ teaspoon freshly ground black pepper

2 cups grated Parmigiano-Reggiano
2 quarts rich chicken stock,
    preferably homemade

Rinse the escarole, trim off the core and any tough or brown outer leaves, and chop it roughly into bite-sized pieces. In a large glass measuring cup, beat the eggs with the salt and pepper just until smooth. Whisk in the cheese until blended.

In a large saucepan, bring the stock to a gentle simmer. Stir in the escarole, and bring the stock back to a simmer. Cook for about 2 minutes. Stir the soup gently in a circle with one hand, and with the other, pour the egg mixture slowly from the measuring cup, drizzling it over the simmering soup as you stir. The egg mixture will form long, lacy strings as it is cooked by the heat of the stock. Use all the egg mixture, but do not stir so vigorously that the egg is completely broken up. Serve at once in shallow soup bowls.

Pasta Fagioli

— SERVES 6 —

Many chefs believe that seasoning should be a multilayered process, and that adding small amounts of salt at several points in a recipe improves the flavor. Here, the presence of two foods that can be intrinsically bland—beans and pasta— dictates that you start with a larger quantity of salt than you would in other recipes designed to serve six people. Then it's up to you to taste, taste, taste.

¼ cup olive oil
1 medium onion, diced
8 cloves garlic, finely chopped
1½ cups dried white beans (cannellini or
    great northern), soaked overnight, or
    3 cups canned beans, well drained
2 cups diced canned Italian plum tomatoes
    with juice

8 cups hot chicken stock, preferably homemade
Fine sea salt and freshly ground black pepper
½ pound tubettini or other small pasta
1½ tablespoons finely chopped flat-leaf parsley,
    for serving
¼ cup freshly grated Parmigiano-Reggiano,
    for serving
Extra-virgin olive oil, for serving

Place a large, heavy pot over medium heat, and add the olive oil. Sauté the onion until softened, about 10 minutes, stirring occasionally. Add the garlic and cook for 1 minute. If using soaked, dried beans, drain and add them now, along with the tomatoes, crushing the tomatoes gently with your hands. Cook for 6 to 7 minutes, stirring frequently so the beans do not scorch. Add the chicken stock, and increase the heat to high. When the liquid comes to a boil, add 1½ teaspoons salt and ½ teaspoon pepper. Partially cover the pot, and adjust the heat to maintain a medium simmer for about 1 to 1½ hours, until the beans are tender but not mushy.

Taste for seasoning and correct if necessary. Reduce the heat to a low simmer.

If using canned beans, add them now to the chicken stock, tomato, and onion mixture. Reduce the heat to a bare simmer.

Warm your soup bowls in a low oven. In a medium saucepan, bring a generous amount of salted water to a boil, add the pasta, and cook until tender. Drain thoroughly, then spoon some pasta into the warmed bowls. Ladle the soup over the pasta, and scatter a little of the parsley and grated Parmigiano on top. Drizzle each portion with a teaspoon of extra-virgin olive oil, and serve at once.

Seasoning is a crucial and widely misunderstood aspect of the larger art of cooking. Try a bite of pasta that has been cooked in unsalted water to understand the blandness that results without salt. Salt allows food to "be itself, but better." That's why even desserts often contain a pinch. Oversalting, of course, can be far worse than undersalting and is not as easily corrected. Keep your mind, as well as your tastebuds, sharp as you begin the process of seasoning: does the dish contain prosciutto, capers, or anchovies? If so, chances are not much additional salt will be necessary. A delicate fish like Dover sole has such an ephemeral flavor that salt could easily overwhelm it. In the Palm kitchens, the briny flavor of the sea is enough.

LENTIL SOUP WITH KNOCKWURST

— SERVES 6 —

"Some of the chefs make this soup with beef, the off-cuts of filet mignon. But I like to put porky things with lentils and beans, so this is my version. The flavor will really improve if you make it the day before." —Tony Tammero, *executive chef*

1/4 cup olive oil

1 medium onion, cut into 1/4-inch dice

1 large carrot, cut into 1/4-inch dice

3 ribs celery, cut into 1/4-inch dice

1 large leek, white part only, well washed
and cut into 1/4-inch dice

6 ounces pork knockwurst or kielbasa,
coarsely chopped

1 teaspoon tomato paste

1 cup brown lentils, rinsed and drained

1 teaspoon fine sea salt, or to taste

1/2 teaspoon freshly ground black pepper

1 bay leaf

Zest of 1 lemon, removed in a spiral with
no white pith

1 1/2 quarts chicken stock, preferably homemade

1/2 teaspoon sherry vinegar

In a large, heavy pot, warm the olive oil over medium heat. Add the diced vegetables and sauté, stirring occasionally, until translucent, about 10 minutes. Add the knockwurst and cook for about 5 minutes, until it begins to color and give up its juices. Stir in the tomato paste, and cook for 1 minute. Add the lentils, salt, pepper, bay leaf, and lemon zest and stir for 1 minute to coat the lentils well. Add the chicken stock, and adjust the heat to maintain a slow simmer. Partially cover the pot and cook for 30 to 40 minutes, until the lentils are tender but not mushy. Fish the bay leaf and lemon zest out of the soup, and discard. Stir in the sherry vinegar and serve at once, or cool to room temperature, refrigerate, and reheat to serve the following day.

SPLIT PEA SOUP

— SERVES 6 —

"If you like a really hammy flavor, sauté the ham with the vegetables." — Brian McCardle,

Palm One chef

4 smoked ham hocks

2 quarts water

1/4 cup bacon fat or olive oil

1 medium onion, peeled and coarsely chopped

2 medium carrots, peeled and coarsely chopped

2 ribs celery, coarsely chopped

1 cup split peas, rinsed and drained

Fine sea salt and freshly ground black pepper

Parmigiano-Reggiano Croutons
(optional, recipe follows)

In a large pot, combine the ham hocks and water, and bring to a boil. Skim the foam from the top, and reduce the heat so that the liquid simmers gently. Cook partially covered for 1 to 1 1/2 hours, until the meat on the hocks is tender. Remove the hocks with a slotted spoon and set aside. Either skim the fat from the stock with a large, flat spoon, or cool to room temperature; then refrigerate overnight and remove the solidified fat layer. Measure out 1½ cups of the ham stock, and freeze the remaining stock for future use.

Warm the reserved ham stock in a large saucepan. Place a large, heavy pot over medium heat, and add the bacon fat. Add the onion, carrots, and celery, and sauté until softened, about 10 minutes, stirring occasionally. Tilt the pan to one side, spoon off as much fat as possible, and discard. Add the split peas and the warm stock, and increase the heat to high. When the liquid comes to a boil, stir in ¾ teaspoon salt and ½ teaspoon pepper. Partially cover the pan, and adjust the heat to maintain a medium simmer. Simmer for 45 minutes to 1 hour, until the peas are tender, and almost, but not quite, mushy. While the soup is cooking, pick the meat from the ham hocks, discarding the fat, skin, and bones. Chop the remaining meat.

Let the soup cool, uncovered and away from the heat, for 10 minutes. In batches, puree the soup in a blender and return to a clean pan (or use an immersion blender). Taste for seasoning, and correct if necessary. Ladle the soup into bowls, and scatter an equal amount of the reserved ham hock meat over each portion. Garnish with a Parmigiano-Reggiano Crouton, if desired, and serve.

Parmigiano-Reggiano Croutons

Preheat the oven to 350°. Slice a baguette about ¼ inch thick, and place the slices on a large baking sheet. Brush each slice with a little olive oil, and season with salt and pepper. Scatter ¼ teaspoon of finely grated Parmigiano-Reggiano evenly over each slice, and bake for about 10 minutes, until golden. The croutons may be cooled and kept in an airtight container, at room temperature, for up to 1 week. Warm in a low oven before serving.

> "I always feel like I have just come home each time I walk into the Palm. Everyone always greets me with a big hello and an even bigger hug. There is nothing better than mixing great food with great friends. The only other thing I can think of wanting is Maurice Chevalier singing "Gigi" from behind the bar."
>
> —Richard D. Zanuck, L.A. Palm regular

MINESTRONE

— SERVES 6 TO 8 —

"This is the ultimate clean-the-refrigerator soup, and the more vegetables you put in it, the better. Don't be limited to the vegetables listed here—just add whatever you've got."—Tony Tammero, executive chef

This soup is even better if cooled to room temperature, then refrigerated for a day. Reheat gently before serving. When seasoning, keep in mind that the ham is salty.

½ cup olive oil
3 tablespoons unsalted butter
1 medium onion, thinly sliced
3 medium carrots, diced
3 ribs celery, diced
¼ pound diced ham
3 cups diced green cabbage
8 cups water
1 smoked ham hock
⅔ cup canned Italian plum tomatoes,
   with their juice
Fine sea salt

1½ cups cooked cannellini beans (drained,
   canned beans are fine)
¼ pound green beans, ends trimmed, and diced
¼ pound zucchini, diced
¼ cup ditalini, conchigliette, or other
   small pasta
¼ teaspoon freshly ground black pepper,
   or to taste
2 cups loosely packed, coarsely chopped
   fresh spinach leaves
⅓ cup grated Parmigiano-Reggiano

In a large, heavy saucepan, combine the olive oil and butter over medium-low heat. Add the onion, and cook, uncovered, until completely softened and pale golden, about 15 minutes. Add the carrots, celery, and ham, and cook for 4 minutes. Add the cabbage, and cook for 5 minutes more.

Add the water, ham hock, and tomatoes with their juice, crushing the tomatoes gently with your hands. Add a little salt, stir gently but thoroughly, then cover and adjust the heat to a very gentle simmer. Cook for about 2½ hours; then add the well-drained cannellini beans, green beans, and zucchini, and cook for about 15 minutes. Add the pasta and cook for 15 minutes more, stirring occasionally. The mixture should be fairly dense. If the minestrone becomes very thick, however, you can dilute it with a little water or broth. Add the black pepper, taste, and adjust for seasoning. Remove the ham hock and let cool slightly. Stir in the spinach and cook for 2 minutes, just to wilt. Pick the meat from the ham hock, discarding the fat, skin, and bones, and add to the soup. Serve with the grated Parmigiano on the side.

SWEET RED PEPPER SOUP

— SERVES 8 TO 10 —

"I like the way the fennel comes through behind the peppers and lifts the flavor in this soup. The jalapeño also adds a nice little sparkle." — Jeffrey Bleaken, Philadelphia Palm chef

1 tablespoon fennel seeds
1 small sprig fresh thyme
1 bay leaf
1 tablespoon dried basil
¼ cup olive oil
1 small onion, coarsely chopped
3 large red bell peppers, cored, seeded,
   and coarsely chopped

1 large jalapeño pepper, stemmed, seeded,
   and chopped
⅓ cup all-purpose flour
¼ cup tomato paste
8 cups hot chicken stock, preferably homemade
1 cup peeled plum tomatoes, seeded
Fine sea salt and freshly ground black pepper
1 cup heavy cream

Place a 4-inch square of doubled cheesecloth on the counter, and in the center combine the fennel seeds, thyme, bay leaf, and basil. Tie into a little pouch with a piece of kitchen twine, and reserve.

In a large, heavy skillet over medium heat, warm the olive oil. Add the onion and cook, stirring occasionally, until very soft but not colored, about 10 minutes. Add the red peppers and jalapeños, and continue to cook without browning until very tender, about 8 minutes more. Stir in the flour and cook for 1 minute; then add the tomato paste and cook for another minute. Add a little of the hot chicken stock, stirring until smooth; then add the remaining chicken stock, the spice bag, and the plum tomatoes. Over medium heat, bring the mixture to a gentle simmer. Stir in 1 teaspoon salt and several turns of the peppermill. Simmer uncovered, stirring occasionally, for about 30 minutes, until slightly thickened. Remove from the heat and discard the spice bag. In batches, puree in a blender until very smooth (or use an immersion blender). Press the soup through a fine sieve, and return to a clean saucepan. Stir in the cream, return to a slow simmer, and taste for seasoning. Simmer for 1 minute more, then ladle into warmed bowls and serve.

GIGI SALAD

— SERVES 4 TO 5 —

Never has a simple dish stirred so much controversy. Rumors are rife, and only the true Palmerati know the difference between a "regular Gigi" and a "West

Coast Gigi." Named for the late, great maestro himself (Gigi Delmaestro, West Hollywood Palm general manager for twenty-seven years), this salad is ordered more than any other single dish at the Palm. True Palm regulars never order "Gigi salad." Just ask for a "Gigi."

1 pound green beans, ends trimmed	*¾ cup Basic Vinaigrette (page 65)*
1 pound ripe beefsteak tomatoes, cored and	*¼ pound bacon, cooked until crisp,*
roughly chopped into ½-inch chunks,	*then drained*
including seeds and juice	*6 jumbo (U-12) shrimp or 12 medium shrimp,*
1 medium onion, cut into ½-inch dice	*cooked, peeled, and cut into ½-inch lengths*

In a saucepan of rapidly boiling salted water, cook the green beans for 4 minutes. Drain immediately, and rinse under abundant cold water until the beans stop steaming. Shake to remove excess water; then spread on a double thickness of paper towels to dry briefly. Cut into 1½-inch lengths.

In a large bowl, combine the beans, tomatoes, onion, and ½ cup vinaigrette. Toss until evenly coated, adding the remaining vinaigrette only if necessary. Mound on chilled salad plates. Crumble an equal amount of the bacon over each salad, and scatter with a few pieces of the shrimp. Serve at once.

> **Variation** for West Coast Gigi: Garnish each salad with a hard-boiled egg, peeled and cut into wedges, and ½ Hass avocado, peeled and sliced.

MONDAY NIGHT SALAD

— SERVES 4 TO 6 —

Remember when Monday night football started back in the early '70s? A guy named Dalessandro used to come into Palm One with a few buddies for dinner before checking into a hotel to relax and watch the game. He eventually started giving the chef advice: "Try a little of this, a little of that in my mixed green salad." After a lot of Monday nights, this salad was requested by so many of Mr. D's friends that it went on the menu. If you're not a big anchovy fan, cut the anchovies by half (then try to learn to love them). If desired, this very flavorful salad can be served with Blue Cheese Dressing (page 64) or Thousand Island Dressing instead of vinaigrette, but it won't be the way Mr. D liked it.

¾ pound mixed greens (iceberg, red leaf, salad bowl, butter, and/or romaine)

2 small radishes, ends trimmed, thinly sliced

3 ripe beefsteak tomatoes, cored and chopped, including seeds and juices

¼ teaspoon fine sea salt

16 oil-packed anchovy fillets, rinsed and chopped

1 small yellow onion, peeled and finely chopped

4 red bell peppers, roasted, cored, seeded, and peeled (see page 182)

½ to ¾ cup Basic Vinaigrette (page 65)

¼ cup crumbled blue cheese (optional)

Wash and thoroughly dry the greens in a salad spinner or with clean kitchen towels (if they are wet, the dressing won't adhere). Chop the greens coarsely and toss in a large bowl with the radishes, tomatoes, salt, anchovies, and onion. Coarsely chop the roasted peppers, and add them to the bowl, tossing gently. Add a generous amount of vinaigrette, and toss again until all the ingredients are evenly coated. Using a slotted spoon, transfer to chilled salad plates, spreading the salad fairly flat. Sprinkle with the blue cheese, if desired, and serve at once.

WEST SIDE COBB

— SERVES 6 TO 8 —

"There was a lunch special that was really popular at the West Side after we opened, a chicken salad with eggs and blue cheese. One day a customer asked me to add avocado, and the people at the next table were looking over and saying 'Hey, what is that?' It kind of snowballed—all of a sudden we're selling fifteen to twenty orders a day. Then someone asked if we could add bacon, and that was a big hit. We decided to put it on the menu, and now, fuhgeddaboudit. It's huge."

—Fabian Nigito, West Side Palm chef

4 (5-ounce) boneless, skinless chicken
  breast halves
½ cup olive oil
Fine sea salt and freshly ground black pepper
8 cups iceberg lettuce (about 1 small head),
  sliced ¼-inch thick
8 cups loosely packed mesclun mixture
2 cups shredded radicchio (about half a
  large head)
1 small white onion, peeled and chopped
  into ¼-inch chunks

¾ pound ripe beefsteak tomatoes, cored
  and cut into ¼-inch dice, including
  seeds and juice
4 small Hass (bumpy-skinned) avocados,
  peeled, pitted, and cut into ¼-inch dice
4 hard-boiled eggs, peeled and finely chopped
8 slices bacon, cooked until very crisp,
  then drained and crumbled
½ pound Danish blue cheese, crumbled
1 cup Basic Vinaigrette (page 65)

Place the chicken breasts in a shallow baking dish, and drizzle with the oil. Season generously with salt and pepper, and cover with plastic wrap. Refrigerate for at least 2 hours and up to 4 hours.

Remove from the refrigerator 15 minutes before grilling. Preheat an indoor or outdoor grill (or a ridged cast iron griddle pan) to medium-high heat. Grill the chicken breasts for 4 to 5 minutes on each side, until firm and completely opaque at the center. Transfer to a cutting board, and let stand for 5 minutes to allow the juices to settle. With a sharp knife, cut the chicken breasts into ¼-inch dice.

In a very large bowl, combine the iceberg, mesclun, radicchio, onion, tomatoes, avocado, eggs, bacon, and blue cheese. Toss briefly, drizzle with the vinaigrette, and toss again until all the ingredients are evenly coated. Using tongs, divide the salad among 6 large, chilled plates, making sure each plate has an equal amount of chicken and avocado. Serve at once.

Variation: Lobster Cobb Wrap
SERVES 6

The Lobster Cobb Wrap is another of Fabian's inspirations. At the Palm, it's served with Cajun French fries, but you can substitute Cottage Fries (page 170), Half and Half (page 168), or store-bought spicy potato chips.

Prepare a *half* recipe of the West Side Cobb salad as above, substituting ½ pound of cooked, diced lobster meat for the grilled chicken. Toss thoroughly. Place six 9-inch black bean or sun-dried tomato tortillas on a work surface, and arrange 1½ cups of the salad mixture in the center of each tortilla. Fold the outside edges in toward the center; then roll the package up from the bottom, nice and tight. Cut the wrap in half, crosswise, on the diagonal. Place one half on a plate lying flat, seam side down, and prop the other half against it, with the diagonally cut side facing upward to show the salad filling. Repeat with the remaining 5 tortillas, and serve at once.

COBB-STEIN

"Norm Brownstein used to come in to the Denver Palm all the time and complain that he couldn't get his favorite salad, some chopped salad that he got at another Denver restaurant. It was basically a chopped Cobb, tossed with a little vinaigrette. I found out exactly what was in it, so I could re-create it. Then we had to name the salad, and naturally we called it a Cobb-Stein. It's not on the menu, but it's very popular with Palm regulars. Chef Joe Profeta still makes the best one, in Denver." —Gerard Quinn, assistant corporate chef

½ pound cooked turkey breast, thinly sliced, then coarsely chopped

¼ pound Swiss cheese, thinly sliced, then coarsely chopped

1 head iceberg lettuce, coarsely chopped

1 ripe beefsteak tomato, cored and cut into ¼-inch dice, including seeds and juice

2 radishes, ends trimmed, thinly sliced

2 green onions, white and light green parts only, finely chopped

½ cup finely chopped white onion

2 cup Basic Vinaigrette (page 65) or Russian dressing

In a large bowl, combine all the ingredients except the dressing, and toss to combine. Add the dressing and toss again, very thoroughly, until the ingredients are evenly coated. Serve at once, on chilled plates.

"It is with great humility that I accept the designation of this salad, and I can only say that it is my favorite dish at the Palm, which is my favorite restaurant. Sometimes, I like to have it with Russian dressing instead of the usual vinaigrette."

—Norm Brownstein, prominent Denver attorney and longtime Palm aficionado

---

ROASTED RED PEPPERS AND ANCHOVIES

— SERVES 4 PALM-STYLE, OR 8 —

Although this dish continues to be called Pimento and Anchovies on the Palm menu, it's now made with roasted peppers. Be sure to core the lettuce hearts without completely detaching the base, so they don't fall apart.

2 hearts of iceberg lettuce, quartered and cored
8 freshly roasted red peppers (see page 182) or pimentos
24 anchovy fillets, rinsed in warm water and patted dry
1½ tablespoons capers, rinsed and drained

½ cup Basic Vinaigrette (page 65), Blue Cheese Dressing (page 64), Jeffrey's Famous Dressing (page 67), Balsamic Dressing (page 68), or Roasted Red Pepper Dressing (page 67)

On each of 4 chilled salad plates, place 2 iceberg wedges and drape 2 peppers on top of each wedge. Lay 6 anchovies across each of the peppers, and sprinkle the capers over all. Serve with the dressing of your choice, on the side.

"This is a classic recipe from Walter Ganzi, Wally's dad. He used to make it with pimentos. In fact, it's only recently we started to substitute roasted peppers."

—Tony Tammero, executive chef

"Pimentos are a little heavier and have a slightly pickled flavor. The roasted peppers give a nice, fresh, sweet flavor to this salad that I like much better."

—Jeffrey Bleaken, Philadelphia Palm chef

CHEF SALAD

— SERVES 1 PALM-STYLE, OR 2 —

"This is Bruce Bozzi's take on a chef's salad, probably the only dish in the book that's his. (He's a front guy, not a chef, even if he is my brother-in-law.) We used

to cut the ingredients in strips, but then he came along and told us to chop, and all of a sudden the salad started to sell a lot more. We use crisp lettuces because field greens may be elegant, but they've got no crunch, no texture. Some people say they'd rather tear lettuce than cut it, because the knife crushes the fibers and makes it wilt. Those people ain't got sharp knives. You've gotta toss this in the kitchen to get the dressing really well distributed. Don't pour on all the vinaigrette at once, cause you can't take it out again if you added too much. There's nothing worse than an overdressed salad." —Tony Tammero, executive chef

2 cups bite-sized pieces of iceberg lettuce
2 cups bite-sized pieces of romaine
    lettuce hearts
1½ cups bite-sized pieces of escarole,
    green part only
¼ pound cooked ham, cut into ¼-inch dice
¼ pound cooked chicken breast, cut into
    ¼-inch dice

¼ pound roast beef, cut into ¼-inch dice
¼ pound Swiss cheese, cut into ¼-inch dice
1 hard-boiled egg, peeled and coarsely chopped
2 green onions, green part only, finely chopped
2 radishes, trimmed and finely chopped
½ cup Basic Vinaigrette (page 65)
Fine sea salt and freshly ground black pepper

In a very large bowl, combine all the ingredients except the vinaigrette and seasonings, and toss to combine thoroughly. Add half the vinaigrette, and toss until the ingredients are evenly coated. Taste, adding more vinaigrette, and salt and pepper, if necessary. Serve in chilled bowls.

GRILLED CHICKEN
CAESAR SALAD

— SERVES 2 PALM-STYLE, OR 4 —

This dish has been on the Palm menu for years, because it satisfies the cravings of almost every customer, male or female. First, there has never been a more popular salad than Caesar, and second, when you're dieting and need a little lean protein, what else would you want but chicken? The salad debuted in Philly, *just to see if it would fly, and then went on the core menu. Now it's one of the Palm's most asked-for lunch dishes of all time, countrywide.*

CAESAR CROUTONS:

2 cups cubed French bread (½-inch cubes)

½ teaspoon dried oregano

½ teaspoon finely chopped flat-leaf parsley

4 small cloves garlic, finely chopped

4 tablespoons olive oil

SALAD:

4 (5-ounce) boneless, skinless chicken breast halves, patted dry with paper towels

Fine sea salt and freshly ground black pepper

2 hearts romaine lettuce (use only the pale inner leaves), torn into large pieces

¾ cup Caesar Dressing (page 65)

To make the Caesar Croutons: Preheat the oven to 350°. In a bowl, combine the bread cubes with the oregano, parsley, garlic, and olive oil. Toss thoroughly to be sure each cube is evenly coated. Spread the cubes on a baking sheet, and bake for 10 to 15 minutes, until slightly golden and very crisp. Set aside at room temperature or, if desired, store in an airtight container (also at room temperature) for up to 24 hours before using. Reheat in a low oven to crisp, if necessary.

Preheat an indoor or outdoor grill (or ridged cast iron stovetop griddle) to medium heat. Season both sides of the chicken breasts generously with salt and pepper. Grill for 4 minutes, turn, and cook for 5 to 7 minutes on the other side, until quite firm to the touch with no trace of pink remaining in the center. Transfer the breasts to a platter, tent loosely with foil, and set aside for 5 minutes, to allow the juices to settle. In a large bowl, combine the romaine lettuce with the croutons and just enough of the dressing to coat all the ingredients lightly. Toss with tongs and transfer to plates or bowls. Cut each chicken breast into about ⅜-inch slices, and place the slices around the edges of each salad. Serve at once.

"These are the power centers of Washington: the White House, the Senate, the House of Representatives, the Palm. The Palm? What you can smell here is *not* the steak and fries, it's money. It is influence . . ."

Morley Safer, CBS News 60 Minutes, February 28, 1999, "The Lobbyist"

Blackened Filet Spinach Salad

— Serves 2 Palm-style, or 4 —

"There are a lot of people, including the author of this book, who, if they can't use an outdoor grill, like to sear steaks in a cast iron pan, because it gets so hot. But I think cast iron gives an 'off,' slightly metallic taste, so I always go for the heavy cast aluminum pans, like All-Clad." —Tony Tammero, executive chef

1 small red onion, ends trimmed
8 small white button mushrooms, brushed
   clean and stems removed
5 tablespoons olive oil
1 tablespoon red wine vinegar
Fine sea salt and freshly ground black pepper
2 (8-ounce) USDA Prime tenderloin
   (filet mignon) steaks, about 1¾ inches
   thick, at room temperature

⅓ cup Jeffrey's Blackening Spice (page 78), or
   Paul Prudhomme's Magic Seasoning blend
10 ounces large, flat-leaf spinach
   (not baby spinach) well washed,
   well dried, and stemmed
1 cup Ranch Dressing (page 66)

Slice the onion in half lengthwise through the root end. Place the halves cut side down, and slice lengthwise into very thin julienne. Thinly slice the mushrooms. In a very large bowl, whisk together 4 tablespoons of the olive oil, the vinegar, ¼ teaspoon salt, and a few turns of the peppermill. Set aside the onions, mushrooms, and vinaigrette.

Preheat the oven to 375°. Pat the steaks dry with paper towels. Spread the Blackening Spice on a plate, and dredge each steak in the spice, coating all sides well.

Place a large, heavy sauté pan over medium-high heat, and add the remaining tablespoon of olive oil. When the oil is very hot, but not smoking, add the steaks and sear for about 2 minutes per side, turning them over with tongs every minute or so. Tilt the pan to one side and spoon off the oil; then place the pan in the oven and finish cooking for about 4 minutes, for medium-rare (if your steaks are not as thick as the ones at the Palm, they may take a little less time to cook). Transfer the steaks to a warm plate, and let stand for 10 minutes in a warm place.

While the steaks are resting, add the mushrooms to the bowl of vinaigrette and toss thoroughly. Add the onions and the spinach, and toss again. Using tongs, transfer an equal amount of the spinach salad to each of four plates, and drizzle with about 2 tablespoons of Ranch Dressing.

Slice the steaks, on the diagonal, about ¼ inch thick; you should get about 8 slices from each steak. Fan some of the slices across the side of each salad, and serve at once.

GRILLED BEEFSTEAK SALAD WITH GORGONZOLA, ARUGULA, AND RADICCHIO

— SERVES 2 —

"Lou Tripodi was a very talented chef who helped us open the West Side Palm, and this was his salad. He's since moved on to other things, but we still have this salad. It's fantastic." —Tony Tammero, executive chef

The chefs like to use filet mignon for this dish, because it is less fatty than some other cuts and thus most appealing when served at room temperature. Since filet also has less flavor than, say, New York strip or rib eye, it makes a perfect partner for the earthy richness of Gorgonzola and the tangy bite of the arugula. This is a great way to use up any cut of leftover steak—whether it's your own or one you brought home from the Palm.

2 (5-ounce) USDA Prime tenderloin (filet mignon) steaks, about 1¼ inches thick
Fine sea salt and freshly ground black pepper
¼ cup extra-virgin olive oil, plus extra for rubbing the steaks
1 generous tablespoon finely chopped fresh rosemary
8 spears Belgian endive
4 small ripe red tomatoes, cut into quarters

4 small ripe yellow tomatoes, cut into quarters
6 cups loosely packed baby arugula leaves (6 ounces)
5-ounce head radicchio, leaves separated and torn into bite-sized pieces
¼ cup best-quality red wine vinegar
6 ounces mild, creamy, dolcelatte-style Gorgonzola cheese, sliced

Generously sprinkle the steaks on both sides with salt and pepper. Rub with a little olive oil and the chopped rosemary. Let stand at room temperature for 20 minutes while you preheat an indoor or outdoor grill (or a ridged cast iron stovetop griddle) to high heat. Grill the steaks to the desired doneness, about 3½ minutes for medium-rare (see Touch Test on page 86). Let the steaks cool to room temperature. If using leftover steak that has been refrigerated, bring it to room temperature before preparing the salad.

Arrange the endive spears at 12, 3, 6, and 9 o'clock on each of two large plates. Place a few red and yellow tomato quarters between the spears. In a separate bowl, combine the arugula and radicchio, and season well with salt and pepper. Add the ¼ cup olive oil, and toss until all the leaves are coated. Add the vinegar and toss again thoroughly. Using tongs (or your hands), place equal portions of the salad on each plate, mounding it nice and high in the center. Slice the steaks just less than ½ inch thick, and fan the slices around the salads. Perch a few slices of the cheese atop the greens, being careful not to push them down too much, and serve at once.

CHOPPED TOMATO AND ONION SALAD

— SERVES 2 —

These two salads date back to Dominic's time, in the '60s, when a lot of customers were just looking for something simple to go with a great steak. The Palm was basically an Italian restaurant, but they would ask for something a little off the Italian track, and Dominic (no one remembers his last name) would make it up. (For that matter, there are still a lot of customers looking for something simple to go with a great steak; that's why this and the Green Bean and Onion Salad are still on the menu.)

1 pound large, ripe beefsteak tomatoes, cored and chopped into ½-inch pieces (including seeds and juice)

½ large white, red, or sweet onion, such as Vidalia, peeled and cut into ½-inch pieces

¼ cup Basic Vinaigrette (page 65), Blue Cheese Dressing (page 64), Jeffrey's Famous Dressing (page 67), Balsamic Dressing (page 68), or Roasted Red Pepper Dressing (page 67)

In a mixing bowl, toss the tomatoes, onions, and dressing of your choice until all the ingredients are evenly coated. With a slotted spoon, mound neatly on 2 chilled salad plates, and serve at once.

"Smell both ends of the beefsteaks—you should smell the aroma of tomato on both sides. We get the best tomatoes in the world, from Lucky Tomatoes, grown in Tampa and the Appalachian valley of North Carolina. They grow them specially for us with no gas or anything, but you can always find good beefsteaks at farmers' markets during the summer."

—*Tony Tammero, executive chef*

Buffalo Mozzarella with Tomatoes, Basil, and Extra-Virgin Olive Oil

— SERVES 4 —

For a slightly fancier presentation, reduce 1 cup of decent (not the aged stuff) balsamic vinegar by about three-quarters in a small saucepan; then put it in a squeeze bottle, like the ones used for ketchup and mustard at a hot dog stand. Squirt squiggles and drops of the thickened balsamic on the edges of the plate before serving.

4 large, ripe beefsteak tomatoes, cored
1 bunch fresh basil, washed, dried, and stemmed
12 ounces very fresh buffalo mozzarella,
   sliced ½ inch thick

Extra-virgin olive oil, for drizzling
Balsamic vinegar, for serving

Trim off the ends of each tomato, and eat or reserve the trimmings for another use. Cut 3 perfectly even, ½ inch-thick slices from the center of each tomato. Place 3 slices on each of four plates, in a single layer. Tear off whole leaves of the basil and bruise them slightly with your hands. Place 1 or 2 bruised leaves over each slice of tomato (bruising the leaves releases the pungent acids that contain the flavor). Lay the mozzarella slices over the tomatoes, making a "sandwich" with the basil in the center. Drizzle lightly with extra-virgin olive oil, and serve with the balsamic vinegar and additional olive oil on the side.

"This salad has just a few ingredients, so they better be damn good. Do not salt the tomato, or, for that matter, anything else on the table. Salt will disguise, rather than enhance, the delicate flavor of the mozzarella. A few turns of the peppermill is all that's needed, and even that's debatable. I like to taste the tomato, the cheese, and the basil, and that's it.

"The only buffalo mozzarella worth eating is made in Italy, in Campagna. There are several brands; just look for Campagna on the label. People have been trying to make it here, but it's no good. Even when they import the buffalo milk from Italy, it's still not right, because there's something about the Italian water. Check the date on the package—keep in mind that buffalo mozzarella only lasts for three days, refrigerated, after you open it.

"If you want to get technical, winter basil from a hothouse has a very different smell than summer basil, and obviously this salad is better with summer basil."

—*Tony Tammero, executive chef*

Green Bean and Onion Salad

— Serves 4 —

1 ¼ *pounds green beans, ends trimmed*
1 *white, red, or sweet onion, such as Vidalia*
½ *cup Basic Vinaigrette (page 65),*
  Blue Cheese Dressing (page 64),

Jeffrey's Famous Dressing (page 67),
Balsamic Dressing (page 68), or Roasted
Red Pepper Dressing (page 67)

In a saucepan of rapidly boiling salted water, cook the green beans for 4 minutes. Drain immediately, and rinse under abundant cold water until the beans stop steaming. Shake to remove excess water; then spread on a double thickness of paper towels to dry briefly. Slice the onion in half lengthwise through the root end. Place the halves cut side down, and slice them lengthwise into very thin julienne. In a large bowl, combine the beans and the sliced onion with the dressing of your choice, and toss until all the ingredients are evenly coated. Using tongs, mound neatly on 4 chilled salad plates, and serve at once.

Hearts of Lettuce with Blue Cheese Dressing

— Serves 4 —

When you make this dressing, it's important to let the cheese and the oil stand together for forty or fifty minutes. That way, the cheese softens and macerates in the oil, and you get a nice, creamy result.

2 iceberg lettuce hearts, quartered and cored
8 (½-inch) slices from the centers of large, ripe beefsteak tomatoes (you'll need 3 large

tomatoes; save the remaining tomato trimmings for another use)
¾ to 1 cup Blue Cheese Dressing (recipe follows)

Place 2 iceberg wedges on each of 4 chilled salad plates, with slices of tomato alongside. Serve with the dressing on the side.

Blue Cheese Dressing
Yield: 1 ½ cups

4 ounces Danish or French blue cheese, at room temperature
½ cup olive oil

½ cup mayonnaise
1½ tablespoons red wine vinegar

Crumble the blue cheese into a bowl and, using a fork, whisk in the olive oil. Let stand for about 40 minutes. Whisk in the mayonnaise and vinegar. Whisk again just before serving.

"I like a salad and an entrée. In the old days, we did it the European way—you got your salad at the end."

—Tony Tammero, executive chef

Basic Vinaigrette

— Yield: 1 cup —

¼ cup good-quality red wine vinegar

1 clove garlic, pressed

Scant 1 teaspoon fine sea salt

¾ cup extra-virgin olive oil

Combine the ingredients in a jar that will seal tightly, and shake vigorously to emulsify. The dressing can be kept, refrigerated, for up to 10 days. Once it has been refrigerated, let stand at room temperature for 10 minutes before shaking so the olive oil will flow. Always shake well again just before tossing with a salad.

Caesar Dressing

— Yield: 1 pint —

Back in 1968, Tony Tammero spent four weeks perfecting this dressing. Considering the spectacular popularity of Caesar salad, and the fact that many restaurants are judged by the quality of their Caesars, this was an important undertaking. In the Palm restaurants, this dressing is prepared in two steps: the initial mixture is made in a large food processor, and then the flavor base is transferred to a standing mixer, where the oil is added gently. (Tony feels the food processor is too violent for this smooth and creamy dressing).

With the smaller quantities used here, however, we've found that whisking by hand yields the best, creamiest result. If possible, make this dressing a day ahead so that the flavors have a chance to marry.

1 large egg yolk (see Note)

½ ounce garlic (3 large cloves), pressed

5 fillets of Spanish anchovy, well washed, drained, and minced to a paste

2 teaspoons Colman's dry mustard

2 tablespoons Dijon mustard

1 tablespoon Worcestershire sauce

1 tablespoon fresh lemon juice

1 teaspoon red wine vinegar

¼ teaspoon Tabasco sauce

1½ cups olive oil

In a large bowl, combine the egg yolk, garlic, anchovies, dry and Dijon mustards, Worcestershire sauce, lemon juice, vinegar, and Tabasco. Whisk until smooth. Place the bowl on a folded kitchen towel to keep it from skittering across the counter as you whisk. Whisking with one hand, use the other hand to slowly drizzle in the olive oil, in a thin stream. Continue whisking until the dressing is completely emulsified. Let stand at room temperature for at least 1 hour, to allow the flavors to marry (or place in an airtight container, and refrigerate for up to 24 hours). Taste for seasoning and, if necessary, add a little more lemon juice and/or vinegar to achieve the perfect balance of acidity.

Note: For the elderly, the very young, pregnant women, and those with compromised immune systems, it is advisable to coddle the egg: place in a small saucepan and cover with cold water. Over high heat, bring to a boil and simmer for 1 minute. Remove with a slotted spoon, and proceed to use the yolk as directed. Or, if salmonella is a concern in your area, omit the yolk entirely.

RANCH DRESSING

— YIELD: 1 ⅓ CUPS —

1 teaspoon garlic salt
¾ cup buttermilk
2½ tablespoons fresh lime juice
1 tablespoon finely chopped fresh cilantro
1 tablespoon finely snipped fresh chives

2 teaspoons finely chopped flat-leaf parsley
¼ teaspoon white pepper, preferably freshly ground
¼ cup mayonnaise (optional)
Fine sea salt

In a mixing bowl, whisk together the garlic salt, buttermilk, lime juice, cilantro, chives, parsley, and white pepper. If desired, whisk in the mayonnaise. Taste for seasoning, and adjust with salt and white pepper, if necessary. Use as desired, or cover tightly and refrigerate for up to 1 week. The flavor of the dressing will improve after 1 day in the refrigerator.

Jeffrey's Famous Dressing

— Yield: 1¼ cups —

"When I worked with Sang a long time ago, he used to pull the tail meat off the ducks we had roasted and put it together with crab, shrimp, and romaine. He made a dressing like this, and ate it for his lunch. We added chow mein noodles as a topping, and suddenly it was a really great dish. In the kitchen, we used to call it 'Sang's duck-ass salad.' I knew I wanted to use that dressing for something, and then I decided to put balsamic vinegar in it. Somehow, it became Jeffrey's Famous Dressing, but it really started with Sang. I put it on my Spicy Swordfish Salad, and it became a hit." —Jeffrey Bleaken, Philadelphia Palm chef

2 tablespoons Dijon mustard
4 teaspoons balsamic vinegar
4 tablespoons soy sauce
1 tablespoon fresh lemon juice

2 teaspoons Colman's dry mustard
3 cloves garlic, pressed
¾ cup olive oil

In a large bowl, combine the Dijon, vinegar, soy sauce, lemon juice, dry mustard, and garlic. Whisk until smooth. Place the bowl on a folded kitchen towel to keep it from skittering across the counter as you whisk. Whisking with one hand, use the other hand to slowly drizzle in the olive oil, in a thin stream. Continue whisking until the dressing is completely emulsified. Let stand at room temperature for 1 hour, to allow the flavors to marry.

Roasted Red Pepper Dressing

— Yield: 2 cups —

2 red bell peppers, halved, cored, and seeded
2 cloves garlic, crushed with the side of
 a large, heavy knife
2 tablespoons olive or canola oil
Fine sea salt and freshly ground black pepper
⅓ cup red wine vinegar

1 tablespoon balsamic vinegar
1 teaspoon sugar
½ teaspoon Cajun spice or chile powder
¼ cup loosely packed basil leaves
½ cup extra-virgin olive oil

Preheat the oven to 250°. In a roasting pan, toss the peppers with the crushed garlic and olive oil. Season with salt and pepper, and roast for about 2 hours, until blistered and completely tender. In a blender, combine the roasted peppers, oil, and garlic, the vinegars, sugar, Cajun spice, and basil. Blend to a puree; then add the olive oil and blend again just until smooth. Do not overblend, or the dressing may break. Taste for seasoning.

BALSAMIC DRESSING

— YIELD: 1¾ CUPS —

Dip your measuring spoon into very hot water for 30 seconds before measuring honey—it will flow much more easily. This dressing is served with grilled vegetables or as a choice with any of the tossed or arranged salads.

1 small shallot, very finely chopped
2 tablespoons soy sauce
3 tablespoons honey
½ cup Dijon mustard
¼ cup balsamic vinegar

Pinch of fine sea salt
Generous grinding of black pepper
½ cup extra-virgin olive oil
½ teaspoon red wine vinegar (optional)

In a large bowl, whisk together the shallot, soy sauce, honey, mustard, balsamic vinegar, salt, and pepper. Place the bowl on a folded kitchen towel to keep it from skittering across the counter as you whisk. Whisking with one hand, use the other hand to slowly drizzle in the olive oil, in a thin stream. Continue whisking until the mixture is completely emulsified. Let stand at room temperature for 1 hour, to allow the flavors to marry. Taste for seasoning and, if desired, add the red wine vinegar to balance the acidity.

— CHAPTER 3 —

Seafood

"I prefer to undercook fish and seafood. That way, you can always fix it. If you overcook, you're done: fish gets dry and flaky, seafood gets tough. Never cut into anything to check the doneness, though. You gotta learn how to tell from pressing it—if it's firm, it's done. Or use a meat thermometer. I'm looking for 110° on the inside of fish or seafood, but at home, you might want to go to 120°. You see, I know where my ingredients grew up."

—Tony Tammero, executive chef

"Quality and freshness are the simple keys to great seafood."

—Brian McCardle, Palm One chef

Butterflied Jumbo Maine Lobster
à la Palm

— SERVES 1 OR 2 —

Don't let anyone tell you that larger lobsters are tough. The Palm is famous for massive lobsters, weighing up to 18 pounds (see photo of Wally and friends on page 21). These delicious behemoths have devotees worldwide. One longtime customer in New York City, who frequently visits his family in England, always stops by Palm One to pick up a giant lobster for them on his way to the airport.

Clearwater Lobster, the Canadian company that harvests the giant crustaceans, sells only to the Palm. Fortunately, this recipe works just as well with 1½- to 3-pounders. It's a bit messy in the oven, but well worth the effort. If you're going to eat the lobster right away, you can dispense with the step of wrapping and refrigerating, but getting the broiling done ahead of time makes things easy on the cook at the last minute, and the damp paper towels really help keep the meat moist.

1½ to 3-pound Maine lobster, alive and preferably kicking
2 tablespoons heavy cream

Warm Clarified Butter (page 32), for serving
½ lemon, for serving

Preheat the broiler to high heat. Place the lobster on a work surface with the belly facing up and the head closest to you. Using a large chef's knife, cut down through the head but not through the hard, rounded shell. Turn the lobster around so that the tail is facing you and cut down to, but *not* through, the shell. Cut or twist off the claws close to the body, and reserve in the refrigerator. Pull out and discard the two little air sacs inside the head, as well as the intestinal vein that runs down the center of the tail. Leave the green tomalley inside.

Brush the exposed lobster meat with the cream, and place the lobster, shell side down, on a baking sheet. Weight the tail with a heavy fireproof object, such as a clean rock or a metal meat mallet, to keep it from curling up. Broil, close to the heat source, for 2 to 3 minutes, until the shell is just beginning to brown.

Let the lobster cool to room temperature, remove the weight, and then wrap in damp paper towels. Refrigerate for at least 1 hour, and up to 4 hours. Remove from the refrigerator 1 hour before serving. Preheat the oven to 425°, and bring a large saucepan of water to a boil. Place the reserved lobster claws in the boiling water, and cook for 8 minutes. Drain and reserve. Fill a small roasting pan with hot water, and set on the lowest rack of the oven. Place the lobster, cut side up, directly on the oven rack above the pan of water. Roast until firm, about 8 minutes for a 1½-pound lobster, 15 to 20 minutes for a 3-pounder. To check for doneness, carefully lift the lobster just enough to see the bottom of the shell; when it's orange, the lobster is cooked. Crack the cooked claws, and place on a large platter with the lobster body. Serve with a ramekin of clarified butter and the lemon half.

LOBSTER FACTS

• June and December are the best months to eat lobster. If you eat a lobster too soon after it molts, it may be watery and mushy.
• The vast majority of the world's lobsters don't have claws.
• The largest lobster ever caught weighed forty-two pounds. The year was 1934, and the lobster was about 300 years old.

CRAB CAKES
WITH MANGO SALSA

— SERVES 6 AS AN APPETIZER, OR 3 AS A MAIN COURSE —

Most crab cakes are pan-fried, I point out to Tony when he gives me the recipe. "The crab is already cooked, right? So why cook it in a searing hot pan? You'll just dry it out," he says. "Let the flavor and juiciness of the crab dominate the dish." Try this deceptively simple recipe, created by chef Sang Ek at the Palm in Washington, D.C., and you'll agree. Crab cakes have been on the menu only since 1985, and the Mango Salsa tiptoed in even more recently.

1 teaspoon unsalted butter
3 stalks celery, finely chopped
3 tablespoons finely chopped yellow onion
⅓ cup mayonnaise
½ teaspoon good-quality curry powder
1½ teaspoons Old Bay seasoning
1 teaspoon Worcestershire sauce
1½ tablespoons Dijon mustard
½ teaspoon Colman's dry mustard

1½ tablespoons drained, finely chopped pimento
2 slices firm, close-textured Italian white bread, crusts removed and finely chopped
1 pound lump crabmeat, gently squeezed to remove excess moisture
½ cup Mango Salsa, for serving (recipe follows)
1 teaspoon minced flat-leaf parsley, for serving
Lemon wedges, for serving

Place a small skillet over medium-low heat, and add the butter. Add the celery and onion, and stir. Cover and sweat gently until tender, about 5 minutes. Remove from the heat and let cool.

In a large bowl, whisk together the mayonnaise, curry powder, Old Bay, Worcestershire, Dijon mustard, and dry mustard until evenly blended. Add the cooled celery mixture, chopped pimento, bread, and crabmeat. Toss the mixture very gently, breaking up some of the crabmeat but taking care to leave some lumps intact, until evenly mixed. Using your hands, form into 6 slightly flattened patties and place on a rimmed baking sheet. Cover and refrigerate for at least 1 hour, and up to 3 hours.

Preheat the oven to 350°. Place the baking sheet in the oven, and bake for 10 to 12 minutes, until the cakes are just heated through. Then place under a preheated broiler on high heat for about 1 minute, just until golden brown on top. With a metal spatula, carefully transfer the crab cakes to small, warmed serving plates. Place a generous tablespoon of Mango Salsa on the side. Scatter the parsley around the edge of each plate, and serve at once, with the lemon wedges.

Mango Salsa

1 ripe mango, peeled
2 tablespoons finely diced red onion
1 tablespoon finely chopped cilantro
2 slices canned pineapple, well drained and
    cut into ½-inch cubes
1 tablespoon fresh lime juice

1 generous tablespoon finely diced red
    bell pepper
1 generous tablespoon finely diced yellow
    bell pepper
½ teaspoon fine sea salt
¼ teaspoon freshly ground black pepper

Cut into the mango to locate the position of the flat pit. Cut downward vertically on either side of it to release the flesh; then cut the mango into ½-inch cubes. Trim and cube any remaining flesh from the pit, and discard the pit. In a bowl, combine the mango with all the remaining ingredients, and taste for seasoning. Cover and refrigerate until serving time, up to 4 hours in advance. You may have some salsa left over; it will be fine the following day, but any longer and it will begin to get mushy.

JUMBO SHRIMP SAUTÉ

— SERVES 4 —

"When we opened Palm Too in 1973, a good customer named Bud Gardner came for lunch five days a week. He kept asking for different things, and one time he says, 'I want some shrimps with garlic, but I don't want 'em broiled like scampi.' So I came up with this way, and it kind of stuck." —Tony Tammero, executive chef

28 jumbo (U-12) shrimp, peeled, deveined,
    and butterflied, with tails left on
Fine sea salt and freshly ground black pepper
1½ tablespoons all-purpose flour
1 tablespoon finely chopped flat-leaf parsley,
    plus 4 small sprigs for garnish
½ cup olive oil
7 cloves garlic, crushed with the side of
    a large, heavy knife

½ teaspoon red pepper flakes
½ cup dry white wine
¼ cup chicken stock
4 tablespoons cold unsalted butter,
    cut into 8 pieces
¼ cup loosely packed julienne of basil
    (about 10 large leaves)
1 lemon, cut into 8 wedges, for serving

Heat a large sauté pan over medium-high heat. Season the shrimp generously with salt and pepper. Sprinkle each one with a tiny pinch of the flour, and scatter a little of the parsley on each. Add half the olive oil to the hot pan; when the oil is hot, add half the garlic, half the shrimp, and half the red pepper flakes. Sauté, shaking the pan occasionally and turning the shrimp with tongs, until the garlic and shrimp are golden, about 3 minutes. With a slotted spoon, transfer the shrimp and garlic to a plate. Add the remaining oil to the pan; when it is hot, sauté the remaining shrimp, garlic, and pepper flakes. Return the first batch of shrimp and garlic to the pan, add the wine, and stir over high heat to deglaze the pan for 1 minute. Add the chicken stock, ½ teaspoon salt, and ¼ teaspoon pepper, and simmer rapidly until the liquid is reduced slightly, about 2 minutes. Remove from the heat, and add the butter and basil. Shake the pan vigorously to emulsify the sauce. Remove and discard the garlic. Place 7 shrimp on each plate, and drizzle with the sauce. Sprinkle each plate with some of the remaining chopped parsley, and garnish with a parsley sprig. Place 2 lemon wedges on the side, and serve at once.

Five percent of orders at the Palm every week are for items that don't appear on the menu. To date, no chef has ever said "No" to a customer's request for a particular dish.

CRAWFISH ETOUFÉE

— SERVES 2 PALM-STYLE, OR 4 —

"Some years ago, we had a manager at the D.C. Palm whose father lived in New Orleans. His dad came to visit, and he brought a bag of these special, secret spices they use down there to make etouffée. He said 'Sang, taste this. Can you duplicate this flavor?' So he went away and had a nice visit with his son for a couple of days. Meanwhile I'm trying things out in the kitchen. He came back and tried my dish, and he couldn't believe it. 'This tastes better than the stuff made from the package!' I told him 'It's just a matter of understanding flavors.'" —Sang Ek, Washington, D.C., Palm chef

½ cup Clarified Butter (page 32)
½ cup all-purpose flour

½ large yellow onion, cut into large dice
2 ribs celery, cut into large dice

½ large green bell pepper, cored, seeded, and cut into large dice

½ small red bell pepper, cored, seeded, and cut into large dice

½ cup Jeffrey's Blackening Spice (page 78), or Paul Prudhomme's Magic Seasoning blend

4 cups chicken stock, preferably homemade

1 pound cooked crayfish tails (if frozen, defrost thoroughly at room temperature)

3 green onions, green part only, thinly sliced

1 tablespoon finely chopped flat-leaf parsley

Cooked white rice, for serving

Place a large, heavy sauté pan over low heat, and add the butter. When the butter melts, stir in the flour. Cook, stirring constantly, to make the brown roux for the sauce base. This will take 15 to 20 minutes total. The roux should simmer gently for the first 10 minutes; then, as the moisture in the butter evaporates and the flour cooks out, the mixture will bubble less and appear thinner. Stir almost constantly for 5 to 10 minutes more, watching carefully to avoid scorching. As soon as the roux turns nut brown in color, add the onion, celery, and green and red peppers, and cook, stirring occasionally, for 10 minutes more, until all the vegetables are tender. Add the Blackening Spice, and stir for 1 minute; then add the chicken stock in a very thin stream, stirring all the time. Bring to a simmer, and cook gently for 10 minutes, until slightly thickened. Add the crayfish tails, and regulate the heat to keep the mixture at a very slow simmer. Cook for 2 minutes more; then remove from the heat, and stir in the green onions and parsley. Serve over white rice.

RED SNAPPER CAPRI

— SERVES 4 —

"I started making this dish at the Hedges Inn. It became very popular there, and then we took it to Miami, where Pablo still has it on the menu. For some reason, we never took it on the road, but I love it." —Tony Tammero, executive chef

4 (8-ounce) red snapper filets, patted dry with paper towels

Fine sea salt and freshly ground black pepper

3 tablespoons olive oil

All-purpose flour, for dredging

¼ cup very finely chopped shallots

¼ cup capers, rinsed and drained

2 cups cored and diced fresh plum tomatoes, about 8

¼ cup coarsely chopped basil, about 7 large leaves

½ cup dry white wine

¼ cup balsamic vinegar

½ teaspoon red pepper flakes

1 tablespoon cold unsalted butter (if necessary)

Preheat the oven to 475°. Remove any remaining bones from the snapper filets, and season them with salt and pepper. In a large, ovenproof sauté pan, heat the oil over medium-high heat. Dredge the filets quickly in the flour, and gently shake off any excess. Sear the filets in the hot pan, without disturbing, for about 30 seconds, until pale golden brown. Turn carefully with a metal spatula, keeping the crust intact, and sear the other side for about 1 minute more. Transfer the filets to a platter, and keep warm while you finish the sauce.

Discard the cooking oil from the pan and, still over medium-high heat, add the shallots, capers, and tomatoes. Cook for about 3 minutes, stirring, until slightly thickened and chunky. Add the basil, cook for 1 minute, and then stir in the wine, vinegar, red pepper flakes, and ½ teaspoon salt. Stir to combine; then return the filets to the pan, cover, and transfer to the oven for about 8 minutes, until the fish is firm and opaque at the center. If the sauce seems too thin (this will depend on your tomatoes), transfer the filets to 4 warm plates. Swirl the cold butter into the sauce to emulsify it, spoon the sauce over the fish, and serve.

> **In 1977,** Pablo Vargas traveled from his native Dominican Republic to New York City to join his brother Tony, who worked at Palm Too. On Tony Vargas's recommendation, Pablo was hired as a dishwasher. He soon fell in love with cooking and began reading culinary tomes and taking classes in his spare time. Pablo became salad man, then assistant cook, and then broiler chef. Twenty-one years ago, he was promoted to head chef at the Miami Palm.

BROILED SWORDFISH STEAK WITH CITRUS BUTTER

— SERVES 4 —

Always use swordfish from eastern waters. Eastern swordfish eat more shrimp than those in Pacific and Central American waters, which makes the flesh pinker and richer in flavor. The colder Atlantic waters also yield a superior quality of fish. This dish would be equally delicious with tuna steaks. It's always a good idea to wash citrus fruits before using the zest in a recipe, since they may have been waxed for protection during transit.

CITRUS BUTTER:

1 pound unsalted butter, at cool room
    temperature

1 orange, well-scrubbed

1 lemon, well-scrubbed

1 lime, well-scrubbed

1 tablespoon chopped flat-leaf parsley

Fine sea salt and freshly ground black pepper

4 (7-ounce) swordfish steaks, about 1¼ inches
    thick, patted dry with paper towels

Olive oil, for brushing

Cut the butter into large chunks, and place it in a food processor. With a grater or a zester, remove the peels, but not the white pith, from the orange, lemon, and lime. Add the citrus peels to the food processor, along with the parsley, ½ teaspoon salt, and a few turns of the peppermill. Process, scraping down the bowl as necessary, to blend the ingredients thoroughly. Place a 2½-foot length of plastic wrap on a work surface, and spread the butter down the center, lumping it close together in large dollops. Bring up one long end of the plastic wrap, and use it to gently mold and smooth the butter into a cylinder. Bring down the opposite end, wrap securely, and freeze until needed, at least 30 minutes and up to 3 months.

Preheat a broiler to high heat and, if the citrus butter has been frozen for more than 2 hours, thaw for about 10 minutes at room temperature. Brush both sides of the swordfish steaks with olive oil, and season with salt and pepper. Broil for about 6 minutes on each side, until firm to the touch and opaque at the center. Transfer each steak to a warmed plate, and top with 1 or 2 disks of citrus butter, cut from the cylinder. Serve at once.

BLACKENED SALMON

— SERVES 4 —

The key to searing foods in a hot pan is not to overcrowd them. Otherwise, the food creates steam that can't escape, and you end up poaching rather than searing. If you don't have a twelve-inch cast iron skillet (all serious cooks should—what about hash browns and sautéed potatoes?), which chef Jeffrey Bleaken prefers, use a heavy cast aluminum pan with a stainless steel lining. Nonstick does not work in recipes like this because the pan can't get hot enough to provide a good sear without damaging the nonstick coating.

¾ cup Jeffrey's Blackening Spice (recipe
    follows), or one of Paul Prudhomme's
    Magic Seasoning blends
4 (8 to 10-ounce) salmon filets, about 1½
    inches thick, patted dry with paper towels

2 tablespoons canola oil
4 (¼-inch thick) lemon slices, for serving
1½ tablespoons finely chopped flat-leaf
    parsley, for serving

Preheat the oven to 400°. Spread the Blackening Spice on a plate, and dredge both sides of each filet in the spice, coating as completely as possible. Heat a 12-inch cast iron skillet over medium-high heat. When the skillet is very hot, place the salmon in the pan. Drizzle the oil over the tops and around the edges of the fish. Sear, in two batches if necessary, for about 1½ minutes, until deep golden brown but not burned. Turn and sear for 2 minutes more.

Transfer the pan to the oven, and finish cooking for 7 minutes, without turning. Transfer a salmon filet to each plate. Quickly dip both sides of each lemon slice into the chopped parsley, and place one on the side of each filet. Scatter a little more chopped parsley around the edge of each plate, and serve immediately.

Jeffrey's Blackening Spice
MAKES ABOUT ¼ CUP

Philly Palm chef Jeffrey Bleaken came up with this all-purpose blackening spice mixture. It's a delicious combination, but Paul Prudhomme's Magic Seasoning blend may be substituted in a pinch.

¼ cup Spanish or California paprika
1 tablespoon fine sea salt
2 teaspoons dried oregano
2 teaspoons garlic powder
2 teaspoons onion powder

1 teaspoon freshly ground black pepper
1 teaspoon white pepper, preferably
    freshly ground
1 teaspoon cayenne
1 teaspoon dried thyme

In a medium bowl, combine all the ingredients and mix well. Transfer to a glass jar with a lid, and seal tightly. Store at room temperature for up to 3 months.

HORSERADISH-CRUSTED SALMON

— SERVES 4 —

"I love the pungent flavor of horseradish with the sweetness of salmon. The texture is interesting too—a little unexpected crunch against the tender fish. The majority of salmon that you get today is farmed, but for a short time every spring, you can get Copper River salmon, and it is just extraordinary." —Jeffrey Bleaken, Philadelphia Palm chef

4 (7-ounce) center-cut salmon filets,
    patted dry with paper towels
Fine sea salt and freshly ground black pepper
2 cups fresh white breadcrumbs, from
    a sourdough or French loaf
2 tablespoons prepared horseradish

¼ cup unsalted butter, melted
1 teaspoon chopped dill
4 lemon wedges, for serving
2 teaspoons finely chopped flat-leaf parsley,
    for garnish

Preheat a broiler to high heat. If you have a separate oven, preheat it to 400°.

Season both sides of the salmon filets with salt and pepper, and place them in a roasting pan or on a baking sheet. In a bowl, combine the breadcrumbs, horseradish, melted butter, and ¼ teaspoon freshly ground pepper. Mix thoroughly with a fork. The mixture should be moist but not gummy. Pat enough of the breadcrumb mixture onto the top of each salmon filet to create a ¼-inch crust.

Broil the filets until golden brown, 3 to 5 minutes. Transfer the pan to the hot oven, or, if your broiler is part of your oven, turn off the broiler and set the oven to 400°. Cook the salmon for 6 to 8 minutes, until firm and opaque at the center. Transfer the salmon to heated plates, place a wedge of lemon on the side, and scatter a little of the chopped parsley over the entire plate. Serve at once.

DOVER SOLE MEUNIERE

— SERVES 2 —

In virtually every recipe in this book that involves dredging in flour, the ingredi-ent—whether it's veal, shrimp, or chicken—is seasoned with salt and pepper before it goes into the flour. This dish is the exception. "The flavor of true Dover sole is so delicate that even salt and pepper could obscure it," says Palm One chef Brian McCardle. Unfortunately, fresh Dover sole is quite difficult to find, and even if you do find it, it will be brutally expensive. Substitute rex sole, lemon sole, or even flounder, but if you do, remember to season before dredging. Everardo Avilas, at the Palm in Houston, is the only chef who keeps this classic dish on his menu.

1 cup all-purpose flour
⅓ cup canola oil
2 (8- to 10-ounce) Dover sole filets, patted dry with paper towels
½ small lemon
⅓ cup dry white wine
¼ cup chicken stock

Fine sea salt and additional freshly ground black pepper, if necessary
1 tablespoon unsalted butter, at room temperature
2 tablespoons finely chopped flat-leaf parsley
2 (¼-inch thick) lemon slices, for serving

Place the flour on a dinner plate. Heat a large sauté pan over medium heat, and add the canola oil. Carefully dredge the filets in the flour, shaking off the excess, and place them, skin side up, in the hot oil. Try to place the filets where you want them; if you try to reposition them in the pan before they have had a chance to "seize," they will stick and tear. Sauté until pale golden, about 1½ minutes. With a metal spatula, gently turn and cook the other side until golden, about 1½ minutes more. Remove the pan from the heat and, holding the filets with the spatula, tilt the pan and spoon off some of the excess oil. Return to the heat, and squeeze the lemon on top. Add the wine, and simmer until reduced by about half, 30 seconds to 1 minute. Add the chicken stock, and simmer until reduced by about half. Taste for seasoning, adding salt and pepper, if necessary. Add the butter, and shake the pan vigorously to emulsify the sauce. Remove from the heat, and add a pinch of the parsley. Gently transfer the fish to warmed plates, and spoon the sauce over each serving. Quickly dip both sides of each lemon slice into the remaining parsley, and place one on the side of each filet. Serve at once.

"After Mimi Sheraton's 1976 review, we had to lock the doors, it was so busy," recalls owner Wally Ganzi. At that time, everything was cooked "to order," even the creamed spinach. "Tony took the kitchen out of the Stone Age, and taught them how to prep things ahead of time. Then, we were able to do the volume, 500 covers in 110 seats!"

ROSEMARY-SEARED TUNA WITH
RED WINE AND SHALLOT DEMIGLACE

— SERVES 4 —

*Quality is always important with fish and seafood, and tuna is one place where you
really have to be careful. There are many different grades of tuna available, but you
should go for the best—sushi grade—even though it is expensive. Still, even the best
tuna may taste dry if cooked to more than medium doneness.*

4 (6-ounce) pieces ahi (sushi-grade) tuna,
    about 1 inch thick
3 tablespoons olive oil
Fine sea salt and freshly ground black pepper
¼ cup finely chopped rosemary
3 shallots, finely chopped

½ cup red wine
⅔ cup Veal Demiglace (see Note)
1 tablespoon unsalted butter, at room
    temperature
2 green onions, green parts only, finely chopped

Brush both sides of each piece of tuna with olive oil, using about 2 tablespoons, and season with salt
and pepper. Spread the rosemary on a plate, and gently press each side of the fish into the herbs so the
rosemary adheres.

Heat a large nonstick skillet over medium-high heat, and add the remaining tablespoon of olive oil.
When the oil is very hot, add the tuna and sear for about 2 minutes; then turn and sear on the other side,
1 minute more for medium-rare (quite pink in the center). Cook for 1 minute longer if you prefer the fish
cooked to medium. Transfer the tuna to a plate, and add the shallots to the pan. Stir for about 30 seconds,
until just beginning to color. Add the wine, and reduce the heat to medium. Simmer until the liquid is
almost completely reduced. Add the Veal Demiglace and simmer, stirring, until reduced by approximately
one-third. The sauce will be quite thick. Taste for seasoning; then add the butter, and shake the pan vigorously to emulsify the sauce. Remove from the heat, and return the tuna to the pan for about 30 seconds, just
to warm through and coat with the sauce. Transfer the tuna to serving plates, and drizzle with the sauce.
Scatter the green onions over the fish and around the edges of the plate, and serve at once.

Note: There are two options for obtaining Veal Demiglace, which is made as a matter of course in all
good restaurants:

    1. If you have time, you can make your own (see page 139)—it will last for ages and make many, many
dinners taste quite wonderful.

    2. Gourmet shops now sell prepared demiglace in small portions (or to mail order, visit www.vatelcui-
sine.com).

"When making the red wine and shallot sauce [page 81], the key is to start with a good reduction. You must reduce the red wine and shallot together before adding the veal demiglace. Then, you're reducing again, at least by half, to achieve all that great body. It would be a shame to have a beautiful, fresh piece of the best tuna, complemented by the tang of rosemary, and then top it with an indifferent sauce. So don't be afraid to reduce! A little great sauce is better than a lot of bland sauce."

—Brian McCardle, Palm One chef

CLAMS AND SHRIMP POSILLIPO WITH LINGUINE

— SERVES 4 —

"This is a classic old Italian dish that never had pasta with it until somebody at the Palm decided to serve it that way. Albino taught me how to make it a long time ago. If somebody wanted pasta, we'd serve it on the side. You know the Italians usually have their pasta first, very plain, and then the fish course and the meat course. In Italy, you would never see spaghetti and meatballs on a menu. You'd have the spaghetti first, and then maybe you'd have the meatballs. This dish was meant to be served with a big hunk of bread to soak up all the delicious juices. I'm tellin' you, Clams and Shrimp Posillipo wants to be alone." —Tony Tammero, executive chef

Kosher salt, for cooking the pasta
½ cup olive oil
6 to 8 cloves garlic, crushed with the side of a large, heavy knife
20 small clams, preferably from eastern waters, scrubbed clean

3 whole basil leaves, plus ¼ cup julienned basil leaves, for serving
Pinch of crushed red pepper
Two 28-ounce cans peeled Italian plum tomatoes, drained well, core ends removed
1½ cups dry white wine

Fine sea salt and freshly ground black pepper
20 extra-large (U-16) shrimp, peeled
*   and deveined*

1 pound imported dry linguine,
*   preferably DeCecco*
2 tablespoons finely chopped flat-leaf parsley

Place a large pot of water over high heat, add 1 tablespoon salt, and bring to a boil.

Place a saucepan over medium heat, and add the oil. When the oil is hot, add the garlic. Sauté for 2 minutes, stirring occasionally. Do not allow the garlic to burn. Add the clams, whole basil leaves, and crushed red pepper. Cover and cook, shaking the pan gently once or twice, for 3 minutes. Add the tomatoes (crushing them with your hands), the wine, ¼ teaspoon salt, and a generous grinding of pepper. Cover and simmer, occasionally shaking the pan gently, for 10 to 12 minutes, until the clams have opened. Remove the pan from the heat. Add the shrimp, and cover. They will cook very gently in the residual heat of the sauce.

When the water boils, add the linguine and cook for 10 to 11 minutes, until al dente. Just before the pasta is cooked, taste the clam and shrimp sauce for seasoning, and return, covered, to medium heat. Discard any clams that remain closed. Drain the linguine well, and mound into warmed pasta bowls. Top with equal amounts of the sauce and shellfish, alternating the clams and shrimp around the edges of the bowl. Scatter with the julienned basil and parsley, and serve at once.

"I love the Palm. I love the people, love the excitement, love the food. I was once very concerned for the safety of a small woman, when she was served a lobster quite a bit larger than she was! . . . otherwise, perfect!"

—Dom DeLuise, L.A. Palm aficionado

Mutual Respect

Washington, D.C., Palm chef Sang Ek left his native Cambodia in 1972, during the Vietnam War, after two of his brothers were forcibly drafted into the army. He started as a dishwasher at the D.C. Palm in 1973 and for 25 years heard no word from his family in Cambodia. Finally, he got up the nerve to return. He found his mother and tried to convince her to come to the United States with him. She felt that she was too old to make such a big change. Now, Sang tries to go back every year to visit her. In the meantime, he worked his way up from dishwasher to head chef and has had a profound influence on the food at the Palm, injecting Asian spices and techniques into a strictly Italian-American menu.

"Ask Sang about the creamed spinach—he makes it the best," all the other chefs told me. Sang claims he learned just about everything he knows from Philadelphia chef Jeffrey Bleaken back in the early days. Then, later on, Jeff wanted to learn about Asian food and spices, so he asked Sang to teach *him*. This partnership is based on deep, mutual respect for the most important thing to them both: great talent in the kitchen. Sang was best man at Jeff's wedding, and now, when he goes to Jeff's family's house for dinner, they always make him do the cooking.

— CHAPTER 4 —

Steaks and Chops

Chefs at the Palm start with USDA Prime steaks, rub them with olive oil, sear them at high temperatures, and—very important—let the meat rest for a minimum of thirty minutes before finishing them in the oven. Tony feels this allows the meat to relax and the juices to redistribute themselves. Chops are also allowed to rest before serving, for the same reason.

Aging: Most steaks that are generally available have been wet-aged—in other words, sealed in a Cryovac bag for up to twenty-one days. Wet-aging produces a good result, with steak that is far superior to that which has not been aged at all. If possible, though, try cooking a dry-aged steak to discover whether the difference in price is really worth it (opinions differ, even among the experts). But don't try to wet- or dry-age steaks in your home refrigerator, because the uncontrolled temperature and hygiene conditions may encourage bacteria growth.

Doneness: At home, if you are unsure whether a steak or chop is cooked to your liking, use the Touch Test below, and keep records to help you cook with more confidence the next time. Never cut into any cooked meat until you are ready to eat it.

The Touch Test: Let your left hand hang loose. With the index finger of your right hand, press down firmly on the area between left thumb and forefinger to gauge the softness; that is how a blood-rare steak feels, if you press it just as hard. Now make a loose fist with your left hand, and press the same area again. The slightly increased resistance is how a medium-rare steak feels to the touch. Make a tight fist, press again, and you will feel the spring-back of a well-done steak. (As executive chef Tony Tammero says, "Well-done's a trampoline.")

Resting Time: If you were to serve a just-cooked steak as soon as it came off the heat, juices would run out onto the plate as soon as you made the first cut. That's fine, if that's the way you like it, or if your steak must be piping hot. However, for meltingly tender meat that's full of juice and flavor, be sure to let steaks rest, uncovered, on a rack, so the air can circulate freely around them, for about half of the total cooking time. You can make up slightly for lost temperature by serving on hot plates, but ultimately the flavor and texture will be so much better than your usual results that you won't mind a "warm" steak!

Getting Good Meat: "Whenever possible, use USDA Prime, with nice marbling," says Tony. "Certified Angus steak is not Prime. It's from another type of steer that is not graded according to Prime and Choice. It's good too, but not as good as Prime." Frankly, the recipes in this chapter are not likely to yield the best results with standard, shrink-wrapped supermarket meat. Notice the thickness of the steaks that is specified in each recipe, then go to a good butcher or gourmet market, or mail-order a steak. If you do, these guidelines will change your steak-cooking practices forever.

All recipes may be increased exponentially.

New York Strip

"The correct way is to cook this steak is under a super-hot restaurant grill, with the fire coming from above, but of course, most homes don't have that. Otherwise, you have to grill, and the heat comes from below. You sear it on one side, then on the other. The final choice is to pan-sear it. The home broiler is definitely not a choice. It just poaches the steak, takes the blood right out of it, and you end up with gray meat." —Tony Tammero, executive chef

2 (12-ounce) USDA Prime New York strip steaks, 1¼ to 1½ inches thick, patted dry with paper towels

1 tablespoon olive oil
Fine sea salt and freshly ground black pepper

Rub the steaks with the olive oil and let stand at room temperature, uncovered, for 1 to 1½ hours.

Place a large, ovenproof sauté pan, preferably heavy cast aluminum with a stainless steel interior, over high heat. Sprinkle one side of each steak with a little salt and pepper. When the pan is very hot, in about 3 minutes, place the steaks in the pan with tongs, seasoned side down, without touching. Do not move or press down on them (this makes it important to get the placement in the pan right the first time—once they're in, you're not moving them until you are ready to turn). After 2½ minutes, season the top sides with salt and pepper, and gently turn the steaks over. Cook without disturbing for 2½ minutes more. Transfer the steaks to a rack set over a plate, and let stand at room temperature for at least 30 and up to 60 minutes.

Thirty minutes before you plan to finish the steaks, preheat the oven to 425°. Return the steaks to the pan in which they were seared, and finish cooking in the oven for 8 minutes for a warm red center (medium rare), or 12 minutes for a pink center (medium). Cooking to the well-done stage is not recommended.

Let rest for 8 minutes on a rack, uncovered and away from any drafts, and serve on hot plates.

"If I had to choose one piece of advice that will make the biggest difference in results for the home chef, it would be 'Don't touch that steak.' Once it hits the heat, leave it alone until you're ready to turn it, and do that as gently as you'd pat a baby's bottom."

—*Tony Tammero, executive chef*

Prime Aged Porterhouse

— Serves 2 to 4 —

Since domestic broilers just don't get hot enough to provide a good char, most of the steaks in this chapter can be cooked in a heavy cast aluminum pan with a stainless steel interior. But porterhouse, because of its bone, doesn't cook well in a pan, so this recipe is for an outdoor grill only. When cooking steaks, it's very important to fully preheat the pan or grill. If you don't, the meat will steam instead of broiling, resulting in gray steak and a panful of juice, instead of meat that is charred outside, juicy and pink inside. For the same reason, when cooking over charcoal, be sure that the coals have had time to turn gray and become covered with ash. That's when they are at their hottest—not when they are flaming. And don't crowd the steaks, or you'll end up poaching instead of dry-broiling. Be sure to place porterhouse steaks on the grill with the filet side facing outward, away from the intense heat, or that delicate piece of meat will be overcooked by the time the sirloin side is ready.

2 well-marbled, USDA Prime, aged
   porterhouse steaks, 1 to 1¼ inches thick,
   patted dry with paper towels

2 to 3 teaspoons olive oil
Fine sea salt

Rub the steaks generously with the olive oil and let stand at room temperature, uncovered, for 1 to 1½ hours.

Preheat an outdoor grill, with one side at high heat and the other side at medium heat. (This is accomplished in different ways with gas or charcoal grills; follow the manufacturer's instructions. If you hold the palm of your hand over the hotter side of the cooking surface, it should be so hot that you can only keep your hand there for 4 seconds.) Salt one side of each steak, and sear them on the hot side of the grill, salted side down, for 2 minutes. Do not touch or adjust the position of the steaks until you are ready to turn them. Salt the top sides, and gently turn the steaks. Cook for 2 minutes more, without touching; then move the steaks to the cooler side of the grill and continue cooking according to the guidelines below. Do not to cut into the steaks to see if they are cooked; instead, use the Touch Test to determine doneness (page 86).

Transfer the steaks to a rack set over a plate, and let stand at room temperature, uncovered but away from any drafts, for 10 minutes, so that the meat relaxes and the juices migrate back to the center. Serve on hot plates. (If serving 4 people, cut the sirloin and filet pieces away from the central bones, slice each piece thickly, and serve each diner some of each cut.)

RIB EYE

— SERVES 2 —

Because of the bone, this steak cooks best on a grill (follow the recipe for Prime Aged Porterhouse on page 88 and cook nine to ten minutes total for medium). But cooking it in a pan, as below, will also give a fine result. Boneless rib-eye steak, which is more widely available, will take eight minutes in the oven for medium rare, with a warm red center, and twelve minutes for medium, with a pink center.

2 (16-ounce) USDA Prime bone-in rib eye
    steaks, about 1¼ inches thick, patted dry
    with paper towels

1 tablespoon olive oil
Fine sea salt and freshly ground black pepper

Rub the steaks with the olive oil and let stand at room temperature, uncovered, for 1 to 1½ hours. Place a very large, ovenproof sauté pan, preferably heavy cast aluminum with a stainless steel interior, over high heat. Sprinkle one side of each steak with a little salt and pepper. When the pan is very hot, after about 3 minutes, place the steaks in the pan with tongs, seasoned side down, without touching. Do not move or press down on them (this makes it important to get the placement in the pan right the first time—once they're in, you're not moving them until you are ready to turn). After 2½ minutes, season the tops of the steaks with salt and pepper and gently turn the steaks. Cook for 2½ minutes more. Transfer the steaks to a rack set over a plate, and let stand at room temperature for at least 30 and up to 60 minutes.

Thirty minutes before you plan to finish the steaks, preheat the oven to 425°. Return the steaks to the same pan in which they were seared, and finish cooking *in the oven* for 12 minutes for a warm red center (medium rare), or 16 minutes for a pink center (medium). Cooking to the well-done stage is not recommended.

Let rest for 10 minutes on a rack, uncovered and away from any drafts, and serve on hot plates.

COOKING A PERFECT RIB EYE

Palm executive chef Tony Tammero believes rib eye should always be served medium, rather than medium rare. Even the best rib eye, he notes, has a tendency to be stringy and tough when undercooked. This is the only cut of meat that gets *more* tender if you cook it a little longer than medium rare.

PRIME RIB ROAST

— SERVES 4 —

"Just because it says 'prime rib' doesn't mean it's Prime. But we use USDA Prime meat for our prime rib. So it's kind of like a double prime. Most restaurants use Choice to save money, and they think they can get away with it, with all the fat, but it just isn't a good idea. You can try to stretch this to serve five or even six, but as far as I'm concerned, everybody who's eating prime rib gets a bone." —Tony Tammero, executive chef

4-rib USDA Prime standing rib roast, with a thin layer of fat on top, patted dry with paper towels
½ cup fine sea salt

¾ to 1 cup veal, beef, or chicken stock, preferably homemade
1 teaspoon Maggi Seasoning, for coloring the jus (see Note)

Preheat the oven to 425°. Place the rib roast, fat side down, in a large roasting pan, and add about ¼ inch of water to the pan. Coat the bone side of the roast generously with the salt, pressing it in. Roast for 45 minutes to 1 hour, until toasty brown. Remove the pan from the oven, remove the roast, and pour the juices into a small saucepan. Return the roast to the pan, bone side down. Add another ¼ inch of water, and return to the oven. Reduce the heat to 325°, and continue roasting for about 45 minutes more. Add ¾ cup of the stock to the saucepan containing the meat juices and drippings, and bring to a simmer. Remove from the heat.

When the very center of the roast measures 135° on a meat thermometer, remove it from the oven and let rest for 45 minutes in a draft-free place. Pour any juices from the pan into the saucepan with the stock and meat juices, and stir in the Maggi Seasoning. Bring to a simmer; then pour into a heatproof fat separator and pour off the fat layer. Taste the *jus* for seasoning; if it is too salty, add a little more stock. Serve the prime rib, thickly sliced, on hot plates, drizzled with a generous amount of *jus*.

Note: Maggi Seasoning, a sauce made from an extract of vegetable proteins, is popular with Asian chefs and widely available in supermarkets. The Palm has been using it sparingly in *jus* "for years," says Tony Tammero. "It adds a little flavor, a little lift in seasoning and color."

FILET MIGNON

— SERVES 2 —

"Filet steaks are real, real tender, but they've got no flavor. They're great prepared au Poivre (page 94), and I like to roast a whole filet, as long as you sear it in the pan first. This is one of those cases where it would *be nice to have a sauce, maybe a bearnaise. Not on the other steaks, though. Not for me, anyway."* —Tony Tammero, *executive chef*

2 (12-ounce) USDA Prime filet mignon steaks, about 2 inches thick, patted dry with paper towels

1 tablespoon olive oil
Fine sea salt and freshly ground black pepper
Bearnaise Sauce, if desired (recipe follows)

Rub both sides of the steaks with a little olive oil and let stand at room temperature for 1 to 1½ hours.

Place a large, ovenproof sauté pan, preferably heavy cast aluminum with a stainless steel interior, over high heat. Sprinkle one side of each steak with a little salt and pepper. When the pan is very hot, after about 3 minutes, place the steaks in the pan with tongs, seasoned side down, without touching each other. Do not move or press down on them (this makes it important to get the placement in the pan right the first time—once they're in, you're not moving them until you are ready to turn). After 2½ minutes, season the top of the steaks with salt and pepper and turn them over gently. Leave them alone for 2½ minutes more. Transfer the steaks to a rack set over a plate, and let stand at room temperature for at least 30 and up to 60 minutes.

Thirty minutes before you plan to finish the steaks, preheat the oven to 425°. Return the steaks to the pan in which they were seared, and finish cooking in the oven for 12 minutes for a warm red center (medium rare), or 15 minutes for a pink center (medium). Cooking to the well-done stage is not recommended.

Let rest for 8 minutes on a rack, uncovered and away from any drafts, and serve on hot plates.

Bearnaise Sauce
YIELD: 1 ¼ CUPS

Tony likes his bearnaise thick, so it mounds up nicely when dolloped on a steak. Thus, the amount of egg yolks in this recipe is slightly greater than usual. Many books will tell you to make bearnaise and other hollandaise-style sauces in a double boiler, but if you are attentive to the temperature of the sauce, and willing to baby it by moving the pan on and off the heat, it's an easy technique to master. It's quicker this way, too.

1 small shallot, finely chopped
1 teaspoon finely chopped tarragon
½ cup white wine vinegar
3 large egg yolks
5 ounces Clarified Butter (page 32), just slightly warmer than room temperature

¼ teaspoon fine sea salt
¼ teaspoon Tabasco sauce
⅛ teaspoon Worcestershire sauce
1½ tablespoons fresh lemon juice

In a small, heavy saucepan, combine the shallot, tarragon, and vinegar. Place over medium-low heat, and simmer until the vinegar is almost completely reduced. Remove from the heat, and let stand for 5 minutes. Whisk in the egg yolks, and return the pan to very low heat. Whisk the yolks constantly until they begin to thicken, just enough so that you can see the bottom of the pan as you whisk. At this point, you must act very quickly: remove the pan from the heat if looks as if the yolks may scramble—that means it is getting too hot! Begin whisking in the butter, 1 tablespoon at a time, whisking each addition in thoroughly before adding the next. Keep the mixture lukewarm by occasionally moving the pan on and off the burner. Whisk in all the butter; then remove from the heat and whisk in the salt, Tabasco, Worcestershire, and lemon juice. Taste for seasoning, and adjust with salt, Tabasco, and/or lemon juice, as desired. Serve at once, or keep warm for up to 30 minutes in the top of a double boiler, covered, over hot but not simmering water. Stir every

5 minutes to keep the sauce on the bottom from getting too hot. Strain, if desired, to remove the shallot and tarragon, and serve over a perfectly cooked filet mignon.

One popular Palm steak that does not appear in this chapter is the double steak. It's an incredibly thick, thirty-six-ounce New York strip steak. Cooked to medium rare in the Palm's 1,400 broilers, it takes twelve minutes on each side, with an additional 6 minutes to crisp up the fat cap. At home, it's not really practical to cook such a big steak all the way through on a grill or in a pan, no matter how hot.

STEAK À LA STONE

— SERVES 1 PALM-STYLE, OR 2 —

Like many Palm favorites, this dish is named after the customer, Lou Stone, who first suggested it to the chef at Palm One. But don't think that you can just waltz into a Palm, come up with a new idea for a dish, and automatically get your name on the menu. This privilege, reserved for the most faithful regulars, only happens a few times per decade. And the dish has to be really, really good.

¼ *cup olive oil*
1 *large onion, very thinly sliced*
½ *cup pimentos, drained and cut into strips*
Fine sea salt and freshly ground black pepper
1 *(18-ounce) USDA Prime New York strip steak, at room temperature, patted dry with paper towels*

1 *large slice Italian-style white bread*
2 *tablespoons Clarified Butter (page 32), warmed*
1 *teaspoon finely chopped flat-leaf parsley*

Heat a large sauté pan over medium-high heat, and add the oil. Add the onions and pimentos, and sauté, stirring occasionally, until very tender and slightly golden, about 10 minutes. Season with salt and pepper, and set the pan aside.

Following the New York Strip recipe on page 87, cook the steak to the desired degree of doneness and let rest for 5 minutes. While it is resting, toast the bread until golden, and cut into quarters.

With a sharp knife, slice the steak ¼ inch thick, across the grain and on the diagonal. Place the toast quarters on a hot plate, and mound the onion and pimento mixture on top. Arrange the sliced steak around the top of the vegetables, and drizzle with the warm clarified butter. Scatter the parsley around the edge of the plate, and serve.

"I like my filet big, and I like it butterflied, and I like it well done. I pity the chef who disgrees with Mr. T when he wants his steak well done."

—Mr. T., *at the opening party for the Staples Center Palm in downtown Los Angeles, April 2002*

STEAK AU POIVRE

— SERVES 2 —

Steak au Poivre can be made with green peppercorns, as here, or with coarsely cracked black pepper. For the latter, press ¼ teaspoon of cracked black pepper firmly into both sides of each steak before searing; then continue with this recipe, omitting the green peppercorns. If you make this dish with filet mignon, adjust the cooking time per the recipe on page 91.

2 (12-ounce) USDA Prime New York strip
   steaks, 1¼ to 1½ inches thick, patted dry
   with paper towels
1 tablespoon olive oil
4 tablespoons green peppercorns
Fine sea salt and freshly ground black pepper

1 tablespoon unsalted butter
1 large shallot, finely chopped
3 tablespoons brandy
½ cup heavy cream
¼ cup Veal Demiglace (see Note)

Rub both sides of the steaks with a little olive oil and let stand at room temperature for 1 to 1½ hours. In a small saucepan, cover the green peppercorns with cold water and bring to a boil. Boil for 1 minute and then drain. Reserve the peppercorns.

Place a large, ovenproof sauté pan, preferably heavy cast aluminum with a stainless steel interior, over high heat. Sprinkle one side of each steak with a little salt and pepper. When the pan is very hot, after about 3 minutes, place the steaks in the pan with tongs, seasoned side down without touching each other. Do not move or press down on them (this makes it important to get the placement in the pan right the first time—once they're in, you are not moving them until you are ready to turn). After 2½ minutes, season the top of the steaks with salt and pepper, and turn the steaks gently. Cook, without touching, for 2½ minutes more. Transfer the steaks to a rack set over a plate, and let stand at room temperature for at least 30 and up to 60 minutes.

Thirty minutes before you plan to finish the steaks, preheat the oven to 425°. Return the steaks to the pan in which they were seared, and finish cooking in the oven for 8 minutes for a warm red center (medium-rare), or 12 minutes for a pink center (medium). Cooking to the well-done stage is not recommended.

Let rest for 10 minutes on a rack, uncovered and away from any drafts.

Just before serving, melt the butter in the same sauté pan and add the shallots. Cook, stirring, for 2 minutes, until softened. Add the peppercorns, and stir for 1 minute. Place the steaks in the pan, and add the brandy. Stand back and ignite the brandy with a long match. Flambé until the flames die down, shaking the pan gently. Add the cream and Veal Demiglace, swirl to combine, and cook for 2 minutes more, spooning the sauce over the steaks. Taste for seasoning, and serve on warm plates, spooning the sauce over the top.

Note: There are two options for obtaining Veal Demiglace, which is made as a matter of course in all good restaurants:

1. If you have time, you can make your own (see page 139). It will last for ages and make many, many dinners taste quite wonderful.

2. Gourmet shops now sell small portions of demiglace (or to mail order, visit www.vatelcuisine.com).

DOUBLE-CUT MARYLAND LAMB CHOPS

— SERVES 2 PALM-STYLE, OR 4 —

"When you get good lamb—domestic, not Australian or New Zealand lamb, sorry to say—it is so lovely and tender. That's the good stuff. Have your butcher leave a little fat on the bone, because it acts as a self-baster, and then when you nibble on the bone, it's real crispy and tasty." —Tony Tammero, *executive chef*

4 (7-ounce) double-cut Maryland spring lamb
    chops (2 bones per chop), or other domestic
    lamb chops, patted dry with paper towels

1 tablespoon olive oil
Fine sea salt and freshly ground black pepper

Rub the chops on all sides with the olive oil. Let stand at room temperature, uncovered, for 1 to 1½ hours. Salt the bone side of the chops generously, and sprinkle both sides of the meat with salt and pepper.

Place a large, ovenproof sauté pan, preferably heavy cast aluminum with a stainless steel interior, over medium-high heat. When the pan is very hot, after about 3 minutes, add the chops with the concave side of the bone downward (the bone of the chops will form an arch, with the meaty " eye" facing upward). Balance the chops with tongs while you sear them for 2 minutes. Turn the chops to one side, and sear for 2 minutes; then turn to the other side, and sear for 2 minutes more. Transfer the chops to a rack, and let stand for 30 minutes, uncovered.

Preheat the oven to 450°. Place the chops, bone side down, in the sauté pan and roast for 10 minutes, for a warm pink interior. Transfer to the rack for 6 or 7 minutes, and serve on hot plates.

Tony prefers the Touch Test (page 86) for determining doneness of steaks and chops. However, for those who want to use a meat thermometer, 115° yields meat that's "rare with a cold center." Look for 120° for medium rare, and 125° for medium.

LAMB CHOPS WITH ROSEMARY

— SERVES 2 —

Lamb and rosemary have an affinity for each other that can be traced back to the hills and fields of Italy. Some chefs like to add oregano, too, but that's overkill, says Tony. Simplicity is the key.

6 (2½-ounce) single-cut Maryland spring
    lamb chops, or other domestic lamb chops,
    patted dry with paper towels
1 tablespoon olive oil

1 teaspoon finely minced rosemary,
    from 1 medium sprig
Fine sea salt and freshly ground black pepper

Rub the chops on all sides with the olive oil. Let stand at room temperature for 1 to 1½ hours. Rub a little rosemary into both sides of the meaty eye of the chops. Lightly sprinkle one side of each chop with salt and pepper.

Place a large, ovenproof sauté pan, preferably heavy cast aluminum with a stainless steel interior, over medium-high heat. When the pan is very hot, add the chops, salted side down. Sear for 2 minutes, without moving. Salt the tops lightly and turn the chops. Sear for 2 minutes more; then transfer to a rack set over a plate, and let stand for 30 minutes, uncovered.

When ready to serve, place the same pan over medium-high heat. When it is hot, return the chops to the pan and reheat for 30 seconds on each side. Serve on hot plates.

Pork Chops

— Serves 2 —

"Grill it or pan-roast it, but don't bother about the time. With pork, you go by the temperature. Myself, I'm looking for 135°, but for a customer I'm looking at 155°, because with most customers, that's the way they're going to eat it." —Tony Tammero, executive chef

2 (10-ounce) pork rib chops, trimmed and patted dry with paper towels

2 teaspoons olive oil
Fine sea salt and freshly ground black pepper

Rub the chops all over with the olive oil. Let stand at room temperature, uncovered, for 1 to 1½ hours.

Place a large, ovenproof sauté pan, preferably heavy cast aluminum with a stainless steel interior, over high heat. Sprinkle one side of each chop with a little salt and pepper. When the pan is very hot, in about 3 minutes, use tongs to place the chops in the pan, seasoned side down, without touching. Do not move them or press down on them (this makes it important to get the placement in the pan right the first time— once they're in, you're not moving them until you are ready to turn). After 2½ minutes, season the tops with salt and pepper and turn gently. Cook for 2½ minutes more. Transfer the chops to a rack set over a plate, and let stand at room temperature, uncovered, for at least 30 and up to 60 minutes.

Thirty minutes before you plan to finish the chops, preheat the oven to 425°. Return the chops to the pan in which they were seared, and roast for 14 minutes for medium well (or, if you like pork the way Tony does, only 10 minutes). Transfer to the rack, and let rest in a draft-free place for 8 minutes. Serve on hot plates.

VEAL CHOPS

"This used to be just a huge porterhouse-cut chop. I almost like saying veal porterhouse, because it sounds better than chop. But we're thinking of changing it to a rib chop in all the Palms. The sirloin side of the porterhouse can get a little tough, but the rib chop comes out like butter. Meanwhile, I still do the veal rib as a special, sometimes with a little Milanese sauce. There are some great dishes with the rib chop, like the Malfata (page 110). Or, I make a little risotto with fresh rosemary and Veal Demiglace (page 139) and put the rib chop on top." —Tony Tammero, executive chef

2 (12-ounce) veal rib chops on the bone, patted dry with paper towels

1 tablespoon olive oil
Fine sea salt and freshly ground black pepper

Rub both sides of the chops with a little olive oil, and let stand at room temperature, uncovered, for 1 to 1½ hours.

Place a large, ovenproof sauté pan, preferably heavy cast aluminum with a stainless steel interior, over high heat. Sprinkle one side of each chop with a little salt and pepper. When the pan is very hot, after about 3 minutes, use tongs to place the chops in the pan, seasoned side down, without touching. Do not move or press down on them (this makes it important to get the placement in the pan right the first time—once they're in, you are not moving them until you are ready to turn). After 2½ minutes, season the tops with salt and pepper and turn gently. Cook for 2½ minutes more. Transfer the chops to a rack set over a plate, and let stand at room temperature, uncovered, for at least 30 and up to 60 minutes.

Thirty minutes before you plan to finish the chops, preheat the oven to 425°. Return the chops to the pan in which they were seared, and finish cooking *in the oven* for 16 minutes, turning after 8 minutes. This will give you a pink center (medium), which is how most people like their veal. (Tony prefers his a little more rare, cooked for about 12 minutes.) Cooking to the well-done stage is not recommended.

Let rest for 8 minutes on a rack, uncovered and away from any drafts, and serve on hot plates.

CHOPPED STEAK

— SERVES 4 —

"This first appeared on the Palm menu around 1945, when we really started to become a steakhouse, but it wasn't a burger—it was 16 ounces of filet steak, chopped. I'm not a fan of chopping up a good steak, but it's popular in some of the Palms, like Las Vegas. Don't ever let anybody tell you to grind up Prime steak for a burger—it won't be half as good as 80/20 chuck. If your butcher likes you, have him grind it twice, first on the larger plate, then on the smaller plate of the meat grinder. My wife, Janine, won't let me pan-sear these burgers on the stove anymore, because it makes such a mess in the kitchen. 'It's the grill or the street,' she says. She's got a point. I suggest everybody cook these on an outdoor grill."

—Tony Tammero, executive chef

3 pounds ground 80/20 beef chuck (80 percent lean, 20 percent fat)

Fine sea salt and white pepper, preferably freshly ground
2 to 3 tablespoons olive oil

In a chilled bowl, combine the beef with 1 teaspoon salt and a pinch of white pepper. (Don't go overboard on the pepper—you just want a little "zing.") Mix gently; then divide into 4 equal pieces, using a scale if necessary—each one should be 12 ounces. Form each piece into a flattened oval, no thicker than 1 inch. Score both sides of the burgers lightly with a knife, first horizontally and then vertically, cutting no more than ⅛ inch into the meat (this allows the heat to penetrate to the center more quickly). Brush both sides generously with the olive oil, and let stand, uncovered, for 30 minutes.

Preheat a gas or charcoal grill to medium heat. Season one side of the burgers with salt, and place on the grill, salted side down. Do not move or press down on them (this makes it important to get the placement on the grill right the first time—once they're on, you are not moving them until you are ready to turn). After 3 minutes, season the top of the burgers with salt, and carefully scoop up each one with the *side* of a large, flat metal spatula, holding a fork opposite to support the burger. Turn and cook, without touching, for about 4 minutes more for a pink center. Let stand for 5 minutes, and serve on hot plates.

BEEFSTEAK PIES

— SERVES 3 —

Tony Tammero's right-hand man and one of the top Palm chefs in the country, Jeffrey Bleaken, mans the stoves at the Philadelphia Palm (and manages to raise five kids at the same time). He came up with this recipe as an alternative to steak and kidney pie; it's also a good way to use all the fabulous trimmings that are a by-product of serving steaks. If desired, you can freeze the uncooked, pastry-covered ramekins, well sealed in plastic wrap, for up to one month. The pies won't be quite as flaky, but they'll still be really tasty. If you do freeze them, remember to brush them with the egg wash before baking. They don't have to be thawed before baking, but increase the cooking time to 1 hour. The recipe may be doubled.

*1 pound sirloin tips and trimmings, cut into
   1-inch cubes*
Fine sea salt and freshly ground black pepper
Garlic powder, for seasoning
2 teaspoons canola oil

½ cup dry red wine
1 cup Veal Demiglace (see Note), or beef stock
4 tablespoons unsalted butter, cut into 8 pieces
*12 small white mushroom caps, sautéed in
   a little butter until tender*

12 pearl onions, peeled and boiled until tender
1 pound thawed frozen shortcrust pastry,
   rolled out ⅛-inch thick (or use prerolled)

1 large egg, beaten with 1 teaspoon water
   and a pinch of salt

Season the beef generously with salt, pepper, and garlic powder. Place a large sauté pan over medium-high heat, and add the oil. When it is very hot, brown the meat well on all sides, about 4 minutes, turning with tongs to get a nice golden color. Add the red wine. Reduce the heat to medium, and simmer until the liquid is reduced to 2 tablespoons, about 6 minutes. Add the Veal Demiglace, and bring to a simmer over medium-low heat. Cook, partially covered, until the meat is very tender and the liquid is syrupy, about 10 minutes. Remove from the heat, and stir in the butter, ¼ teaspoon salt, and a generous grinding of black pepper. Taste for seasoning, and correct, if needed. Spoon one-third of the mixture into each of three 12-ounce ramekins, and add the mushrooms and pearl onions, dividing evenly. Cut 3 circles from the shortcrust pastry, each 1 inch larger in diameter than the top rims of the ramekins. Cut a ¾-inch vent hole in the top of each circle. Brush the tops and ¼ inch down the outside rims of the ramekins with egg wash, and fit each with a circle of pastry, pressing in around the outside rim to secure. Reserve the remaining egg wash. (At this point, the prepared pies can be refrigerated for up to 4 hours. Bring to room temperature for 10 minutes before baking.)

Preheat the oven to 400°. Brush the top of the dough with a little more egg wash, and bake the pies for 25 minutes, until the pastry is golden brown. Let cool for 5 minutes, and serve.

Note: There are two options for replacing Veal Demiglace, which is made as a matter of course in all good restaurants:

1. If you have time, you can make your own (page 139)—it will last for ages and make many, many dinners taste quite wonderful.

2. Gourmet shops now sell small portions of demiglace (or to mail order, visit www.vatelcuisine.com).

TONY'S SUPERB HOT DOGS

— SERVES 4, CAN BE INCREASED EXPONENTIALLY —

This recipe, though very collectible, is not on any Palm menu. "The neighbors are always askin' me why my hot dogs are so good. They love my food, and when I'm not around they ask my wife, Janine, to fax over my special recipes so they can learn my secrets. Here's my secret hot dog recipe. Be sure to get the hot dogs in the casings, not the skinless ones. Don't toast the buns—they gotta be soft and yielding, so all the condiments sink in and they don't fall apart when you bite into the dog." —Tony Tammero, executive chef

8 Nathan's or Sabrett all-beef hot dogs, with casings

8 egg-dough torpedo or other soft hot dog buns

Kosher mustard, Heinz sweet pickle relish, and sauerkraut, for serving

New York Hot Red Onion Sauce (recipe follows)

Make a charcoal fire in a kettle grill, and let it burn down until the coals are covered with a layer of fine, gray ash. Place a sheet of aluminum foil over the grate, and place the hot dogs on top. Cook for 8 to 10 minutes, until the dogs are just beginning to brown. Transfer the dogs directly onto the grill grate, discarding the foil. Continue grilling until golden brown and crusty, 1 to 2 minutes more, turning to give them nice grill marks. Serve in the soft buns, with condiments on the side.

New York Hot Red Onion Sauce

2 tablespoons canola oil

2 large Vidalia or other sweet onions, thinly sliced

12-ounce bottle Heinz ketchup

1 small (2-ounce) bottle Tabasco sauce

Pinch of crushed red pepper

¼ cup water, if necessary

Place a large sauté pan over medium-low heat, and add the oil. Add the onions and sauté gently, stirring occasionally, until very soft, about 15 minutes. Add the ketchup, Tabasco, and red pepper, and stir occasionally for 10 minutes more, until the onions start to melt into the sauce. Thin with a little water, if desired.

CHAPTER 5

Veal and Poultry

Veal Parmigiana

— Serves 2 —

Veal Parmigiana is a classic red-check-tablecloth dish that can be sublime or indifferent. The fact that it has remained on the Palm menu for generations testifies to the excellence of this version. There's no danger it will disappear from the menu, either. A dish can make up 1 percent of sales for decades at the Palm before it gets axed. The last dish dropped from the core menu was the very old-fashioned (not that there's anything wrong with that) Veal Française, which had been declining in popularity for about 30 years. When the management decided to say goodbye, it was tough. And if some hungry diner today feels like eating Veal Française? "No problem," says Tony Tammero, executive chef.

2 veal scallops, 6 to 7 ounces each,
   preferably cut from the top round
2 large eggs
All-purpose flour, for dredging
1 cup seasoned dry breadcrumbs
⅓ cup olive oil
¾ cup Marinara Sauce (page 130), or
   best-quality bottled marinara sauce

½ cup freshly grated Parmigiano-Reggiano
10 (¼-inch-thick) slices Muenster cheese,
   about 12 ounces
2 teaspoons chopped flat-leaf parsley,
   for serving

Place each scallop between large sheets of plastic wrap on a work surface. Use the flat side of a meat mallet to pound lightly from the center outward, gently easing the veal to an even thickness of about ¼ inch. The scallops should be roughly 8 by 4 inches. (This step may be done up to 4 hours in advance; refrigerate the scallops on a baking sheet, still sandwiched between sheets of plastic wrap, until 10 minutes before you are ready to cook them.)

In a large, shallow bowl, beat the eggs thoroughly. Place the flour and breadcrumbs in two similar bowls, and set all three bowls near the stove.

Preheat the broiler. If you don't have a pan large enough to sauté both scallops without overlapping, cook them in two batches. Do not coat the second one until just before you cook it. Place a large sauté pan over medium-high heat, and add the olive oil. Dip each scallop first in the flour, shaking off any excess, then in the beaten egg. Finally, dredge in the breadcrumbs, making sure both sides are coated evenly, and gently shake off the excess. Place the scallops in the pan, without overlapping, and cook without disturbing until golden brown on the bottom, about 1½ minutes. Using a metal spatula, turn and cook until the other side is golden, about 1½ minutes more. If cooking in batches, transfer to a baking sheet lined with paper towels, and keep warm in a low oven. Otherwise, gently pat both scallops with a paper towel, and transfer directly to large ovenproof plates. Divide the Marinara Sauce between the two plates, coating the veal evenly. Sprinkle the Parmigiano evenly over each scallop, and top with an even layer of the Muenster slices. Place the plates, one at a time, under the broiler until the cheese is melted, bubbling, and golden brown, about 5 minutes. Scatter with the parsley, and serve at once.

Ideally, have your butcher pound veal scallops to save time. Always pound gently but firmly, working from the center outward. Be sure not to break through the delicate meat, and try to achieve an even thickness overall, for more precise cooking.

VEAL MARTINI

SERVES 2

"I wouldn't say we're constantly searching for new ideas, because our customers love the food the way it is—they wouldn't let us change too much. But sometimes you want something a little different. At the East Hampton Palm, I had been working on a different take on Veal Marsala. I'd been messing around with vermouth, but then decided the dish was better with white wine. One evening, I finally got it right, and I looked up to see a guy sitting at the bar with a martini. That's how this dish got its name." —Tony Tammero, executive chef

¾ pound veal scallops, preferably cut from
   the top round
½ cup dry white wine
¼ cup dry-pack sun-dried tomatoes
   (about 4 halves)
2 tablespoons olive oil

Fine sea salt and freshly ground black pepper
All-purpose flour, for dredging
1½ tablespoons finely chopped shallots
3 ounces shiitake mushrooms, stemmed,
   wiped clean, and thinly sliced

3 ounces white button mushrooms, stemmed,
    wiped clean, and thinly sliced

1 small roma or plum tomato, seeded,
    and cut into ¼-inch dice
4 basil leaves, cut into julienne

⅓ cup marsala
2 tablespoons Veal Demiglace (optional, see Note)

3 tablespoons cold unsalted butter,
    cut into 6 pieces

Place each scallop between large sheets of plastic wrap on a work surface. Use the flat side of a meat mallet to pound lightly from the center outward, gently easing the veal to an even thickness, about ¼ inch. The scallops should be roughly 8 by 4 inches. (This step may be done up to 4 hours in advance; refrigerate the scallops on a baking sheet, still sandwiched between sheets of plastic wrap, until 10 minutes before you are ready to cook them.)

Warm the wine in a small saucepan. Remove it from the heat, and add the sun-dried tomatoes. Let stand for 20 minutes to rehydrate. Drain, reserving the wine, and press or squeeze the tomatoes to remove excess liquid. Slice into julienne strips. Place a large sauté pan over medium-high heat, and add the olive oil.

Salt and pepper both sides of the veal. On a plate, spread a generous amount of flour for dredging. Dredge each scallop in the flour, and shake off the excess. Add the veal to the pan, and sauté for 1 minute; then turn the veal and add the shallots. Cook for 1 minute, and add the sun-dried tomatoes, shiitakes, and button mushrooms. Reduce the heat slightly, and cook for 2 minutes more, stirring occasionally. Add the reserved white wine and the marsala, and simmer until the vegetables are tender, about 3 minutes. Add the Veal Demiglace, ½ teaspoon fine sea salt, and 7 to 8 turns of the peppermill, and simmer for 1 to 2 minutes more, until most, but not all, of the liquid has been absorbed. Remove the pan from the heat, and add the tomato, basil, and butter. Swirl the pan until the butter is melted, and serve at once.

Note: There are two options for Veal Demiglace, which is made as a matter of course in all good restaurants:

1. If you have time, you can make your own (page 139)—it will last for ages and make many, many dinners taste quite wonderful.

2. Gourmet shops now sell small portions of demiglace (or to mail order, visit www.vatelcuisine.com).

"We keep the veal dishes on the menu because that's what the Palm was about in the early days, and it's part of the heritage. We could save a lot of money by just concentrating on steak and lobster, but that's not the Palm way. For one thing, Pio Bozzi and John Ganzi would turn over in their graves."

—Tony Tammero, executive chef

VEAL MILANESE

At the Palm, this classic is always crisp on the outside, with a delicate crust, and juicy inside—a perfect, simple expression of the old way with veal. At home, you can duplicate this superb longtime favorite only by waiting until the butter/oil mixture is sufficiently hot before dredging the scallops in flour and breadcrumbs. Dredge too soon, and the result will be soggy and unappetizing.

2 veal scallops (4 to 5 ounces each), preferably cut from the top round
2 large eggs
All-purpose flour, for dredging
1 cup seasoned dry breadcrumbs
3 tablespoons Clarified Butter (page 32)
3 tablespoons olive oil

1 tablespoon unsalted butter, at room temperature
2 (¼-inch) lemon slices, for garnish
2 tablespoons finely chopped flat-leaf parsley, for garnish
1 lemon, cut into 8 wedges, for serving

Place each scallop between large sheets of plastic wrap on a work surface. Use the flat side of a meat mallet to pound lightly from the center outward, gently easing the veal to an even thickness, about ¼ inch. The scallops should be roughly 3 by 5 inches. (This step may be done up to 4 hours in advance; refrigerate the scallops on a baking sheet, still sandwiched between sheets of plastic wrap, until 10 minutes before you are ready to cook them.)

In a large, shallow bowl, beat the eggs. Place the flour and breadcrumbs separately in two similar bowls, and set all three bowls near the stove.

In a large sauté pan, heat the clarified butter and olive oil over medium-high heat until sizzling. Dip each scallop first in the flour, shaking off any excess, and then in the beaten egg. Finally, dredge in the breadcrumbs, making sure both sides are coated evenly, and gently shake off the excess. Place the scallops in the pan without overlapping, and cook without disturbing until golden brown on the bottom, about 1½ minutes. With a metal spatula, turn and cook until the other side is golden, about 1½ minutes more. Transfer to paper towels, and pat gently to blot excess oil.

Drain off and discard the oil from the pan. With the pan off the heat, add the butter and swirl until the heat of the pan melts it. Transfer the veal to warm plates, and drizzle with a little of the melted butter. Quickly dip both sides of each lemon slice into the chopped parsley, and place one in the center of each scallop. Scatter a little more chopped parsley around the edges of the plates, and serve immediately, with lemon wedges on the side.

"There's a lot of variation in quality with veal. We use the perfect stuff: naturally fed, pink and white, none of this red meat that comes from an older calf. And the younger the veal, the leaner the meat. That's why veal doesn't sear as well as beef—there's no marbling. Sure, it takes me extra time to train the chefs to do these dishes correctly. But if we're going to do it, we're going to do it right."

—Tony Tammero, executive chef

VEAL PICCATA

— SERVES 2 —

Piccata is one trattoria classic that is also a true Italian tradition, not just an American invention. In fact, it is such a part of the Italian food culture that some rather profound variations on the dish show up on restaurant menus from region to region. In northern Italy, for example, veal piccata will not contain capers, whereas in the south, capers are a given. The Palm serves a northern Italian version, of course, since the original, influential chefs were from Parma.

6 veal scallops (2 ounces each), preferably
  cut from the top round
All-purpose flour, for dredging
⅓ cup olive oil
Fine sea salt and white pepper, preferably
  freshly ground
1 lemon, halved

¼ cup dry white wine
¼ cup chicken stock
2 tablespoons unsalted butter, at room
  temperature
2 (¼-inch) lemon slices, for garnish
1 tablespoon finely chopped flat-leaf parsley,
  for garnish

Place each scallop between large sheets of plastic wrap on a work surface. Use the flat side of a meat mallet to pound lightly from the center outward, gently easing the veal to an even thickness, about ¼ inch. The scallops should be roughly 3 inches in diameter. (This step may be done up to 4 hours in advance; refrigerate the scallops on a baking sheet, still sandwiched between the sheets of plastic wrap, until 10 minutes before you are ready to cook them.)

On a plate, spread a generous amount of flour for dredging. Place a large sauté pan over high heat, and add the olive oil. Season the scallops on both sides with salt and white pepper, and dredge thoroughly in the flour, shaking off the excess. If you don't have a pan large enough to sauté all the scallops without overlapping, cook them in two batches. Do not dredge the second batch in flour until just before you cook it.

Cook the scallops undisturbed until they are light golden brown and you see the juices begin to run on the top, about 30 seconds. Using tongs, turn and cook for another 20 seconds or so, until golden on the other side. Pour off the excess oil. Squeeze the juice from the lemon halves into the pan; then add the lemon halves and wine, and simmer until almost completely evaporated. Add the chicken stock and salt and pepper to taste, and simmer until the sauce is slightly thickened, about 3 minutes. Remove the pan from the heat, and swirl in the butter, shaking the pan vigorously until the sauce is emulsified. Transfer three scallops to each warmed plate and, using a fine sieve, strain an equal amount of the pan sauce over each. Quickly dip both sides of each lemon slice into the chopped parsley, and place one in the center of each plate. Scatter a little more chopped parsley around the edges of the plates, and serve immediately.

VEAL MARSALA

— SERVES 2 —

"During my early years at the Palm, my favorite chef, Albino Serpaglia, would run this dish as a special. It was incredibly popular. Sometimes he used veal, and sometimes he would make chicken Marsala. I swear, Albino could bone out a chicken in one minute." —Tony Tammero, executive chef

6 veal scallops (2 ounces each), preferably cut from the top round
All-purpose flour, for dredging
2 tablespoons canola oil
2 tablespoons olive oil
Fine sea salt and white pepper, preferably freshly ground

8 ounces white button mushrooms, thinly sliced
¾ cup marsala
1 cup Veal Demiglace (see Note)
2 tablespoons unsalted butter, at room temperature
1 tablespoon finely chopped flat-leaf parsley, for garnish

Place each scallop between large sheets of plastic wrap on a work surface. Use the flat side of a meat mallet to pound lightly from the center outward, gently easing the veal to an even thickness, about ¼ inch. The scallops should be roughly 3 inches in diameter. (This step may be done up to 4 hours in advance; refrigerate the scallops on a baking sheet, still sandwiched between sheets of plastic wrap, until 10 minutes before you are ready to cook them.)

On a plate, spread a generous amount of flour for dredging.

In a large sauté pan, heat the canola oil and the olive oil over high heat. Season the scallops on both sides with salt and white pepper, and dredge thoroughly in the flour, shaking off the excess. Add the veal to the pan, and sauté for about 1½ minutes, until slightly golden. Using tongs, turn the scallops and add the mushrooms. Cook for about 2 minutes, until the scallops are golden on the bottom. Tip the pan to spoon off as much of the cooking oil as possible. Place the veal scallops on top of the mushrooms, and add the marsala. Simmer for about 2 minutes; the mixture will still be quite juicy. Add the Veal Demiglace, and continue to simmer, shaking the pan occasionally, until the sauce is slightly thickened, about 1½ minutes. Remove the pan from the heat, and add the butter. Shake the pan vigorously to emulsify the sauce. Transfer three scallops to each warm plate, and spoon the mushrooms and sauce on top. Scatter the parsley over the center and edges of the plates, and serve at once.

Note: There are two good sources for Veal Demiglace, which is made as a matter of course in all good restaurants:

1. If you have time, you can make your own (page 139)—it will last for ages and make many, many dinners taste quite wonderful.

2. Gourmet shops now sell small portions of demiglace (or to mail order, visit www.vatelcuisine.com).

"Contrary to what Larry King said [in the preface], Gigi once picked up my check, in 1984."

—*Asher Dan, close friend of the late Gigi Delmaestro and Larry King, and L.A. Palm regular*

VEAL MALFATA

— SERVES 2 —

In Texas, at the opening of the San Antonio Palm, I convinced Tony to cook Veal Malfata for me. It's one of his favorites, served occasionally as a dinner special; the bone-in veal rib chops must be special-ordered. Several of the top Palmerati were also in town for the festivities and tried to join us, but Tony had only secured three chops, so just two lucky people were slated to join me.

"When it's ready, it's ready. You guys get your butts on the chairs at 7 p.m. sharp, or you can fuhgeddaboudit," said Tony.

We were not disappointed. This dish illustrates the marriage of old and new at the Palm better than any other, and the crisp, biting arugula salad is a fabulous foil for the savory chop. Try to sweet-talk your butcher into giving you rib chops. Since the meat is pounded quite thinly, it could easily dry out on a loin chop; the well-marbled rib meat near the bone takes much better to this method of cooking.

For really crisp arugula, Tony likes to wash the stemless leaves twice, then place them between paper towels and refrigerate for up to an hour before using. If the arugula will be held in the refrigerator for any longer, place the towel-wrapped greens inside a plastic bag and seal tightly.

2 bone-in veal rib chops (12 ounces each)
½ cup all-purpose flour, for dredging
Fine sea salt and freshly ground black pepper
1 whole egg, whisked with 2 egg yolks
½ cup seasoned dry Italian breadcrumbs
¾ cup olive oil

¼ cup Clarified Butter (page 32)
1 large, ripe beefsteak tomato, halved and diced
1 tablespoon fresh lemon juice
Zest of 1 small lemon
6 cups baby arugula (about 6 ounces), washed, dried, and stemmed

Trim off most, but not all, of the surface fat from each chop. Place a chop between two sheets of plastic wrap and pound gently, away from the bone, right up to but not actually on the bone, until the meat is an even ¼ inch thick. Repeat with the other chop, and salt and pepper generously on both sides. Cut two new pieces of plastic wrap, and spread one on a clean work surface.

Preheat the oven to 350°, and place a rimmed baking sheet inside to warm.

On a plate, spread a generous amount of flour for dredging. Place the whisked egg mixture in a wide, shallow bowl, and whisk in a little salt. Spread the seasoned breadcrumbs evenly on a plate. Dredge the chops in the flour, shaking off the excess, and then in the egg mixture, making sure each chop is well coated on both sides. Drain off the excess for a moment; then place on top of the seasoned breadcrumbs and press down. Turn and press again to pick up an even coating of breadcrumbs. Place in the center of one of the new pieces of plastic wrap, and repeat with the remaining chop. Cover with the second piece of plastic wrap, and press down gently to secure the coating to the surface of the meat. Remove the plastic wrap, and salt and pepper the breaded chops lightly on both sides.

Place a large sauté pan over medium heat and add ¼ cup of the olive oil. When the oil is hot, add the

Clarified Butter. To test the temperature, throw in a breadcrumb; it should sizzle gently. Add the chops and cook, without moving, until pale golden, about 2 minutes. Turn gently, and cook until pale golden on the other side, about 2 minutes more. Transfer the chops to a plate, and tilt the pan to spoon off all the fat; wipe it clean with a paper towel. Add another ¼ cup of the olive oil, reduce the heat to low, and when the oil is hot, return the chops to the pan. Spoon the warm oil over the thick bone side of the chops as they cook for about 3 minutes more on each side. Remove the chops and drain on paper towels, gently patting the top dry. Return the chops to the pan, and place in the oven. Roast for 6 minutes, until the meat near the bone is cooked through, for medium.

Meanwhile, in a bowl, combine the tomato, lemon juice, lemon zest, ¼ teaspoon salt, and a few turns of the peppermill; toss well. Remove the chops from the oven, and tent the pan loosely with foil. Add the arugula and the remaining ¼ cup olive oil to the tomato mixture, toss gently, and taste for seasoning. Mound half the salad on each plate, and place a chop on top. Serve at once.

ZESTING LEMONS

There are two practical choices for this task. You can use a very sharp, swivel-bladed vegetable peeler to remove strips of the zest *only* (leaving the white pith behind). Pile several strips together, and cut into fine julienne; then turn 90 degrees and cut into very fine dice. But obtaining the flavorful lemon zest is much easier with the tool made for that purpose—called, not unreasonably, a zester. It has sharp little eyelets across the top and will produce very fine shreds of pithless zest from any well-washed and dried lemon in less than half the time of the first method.

CHICKEN BRUNO

— SERVES 3 PALM-STYLE, OR 4 —

This dish is no longer on the core Palm menu, and many of the new chefs have never made it or even heard of it. But if you find a nice, old-school Palm chef, he might make it especially for you. It appears here as a favor to my friend Laurie

Burrows Grad and her husband, Peter Grad. ("Bruno is God dressed in crispy skin," muses Peter.) Their likenesses, along with that of their son, Nick, appear on the wall at the West Hollywood Palm.

2½-pound chicken, preferably free-range,
  cut into 18 pieces (2 wings, 4 pieces from
  each breast, and 4 pieces from each leg)
Fine sea salt and freshly ground black pepper
3 large eggs

All-purpose flour, for dredging
1½ cups seasoned dry Italian breadcrumbs
3 cups canola oil, for frying
¼ cup unsalted butter, melted (optional)

Season the chicken pieces generously on all sides with salt and pepper. In a large, shallow bowl, beat the eggs. Place the flour and breadcrumbs in two similar bowls, and set all three bowls near the stove. Place a large sauté pan over medium-high heat, and add about 1½ inches of oil. Dredge the chicken pieces first in the flour, then in the egg, and finally in the breadcrumbs, letting any excess fall away. When the oil is hot but not smoking, add about 7 pieces of chicken (do not crowd the pan; leave ¾ inch of space between each piece). Pan-fry without disturbing for about 3 minutes, until golden brown on the bottom. Using long-handled tongs, turn and continue cooking until all the pieces are an even, deep golden brown on all sides, about 3 minutes more. As the chicken is done, transfer it to a baking sheet lined with paper towels and repeat with the remaining chicken. Keep the browned chicken warm in a low oven while you pan-fry the remainder. Serve at once, on warmed plates. For a delicious option, pour off the cooking oil from the pan and add the melted butter. Gently return the cooked chicken pieces to the pan over medium heat, and turn carefully (so as not to disturb the crust) until coated with butter.

"In the old days, we had a lot of different chicken dishes on the menu: Cordon Bleu, stuffed, roasted, Bruno, Française. We used to bone out all our chickens and make those breasts with the wing attached. The rest of the bones went into stock and soups. We even boned out hindsaddles of veal—and they could weigh 100, 125 pounds. Today, you give a chef a hindsaddle of veal, and I promise you he won't know what to do with it. Even some of the guys in the market don't know how to do it. In the old days, the kitchen guys learned from the ground up. The meat came in on the hook. Now, everything comes perfectly precut because we don't have the time or the training in the kitchen. We even have to buy the bones for our stocks and soups. What's that about? I guess it's progress."

—*Tony Tammero, executive chef*

BLACKENED CHICKEN

— SERVES 4 —

"I recently read in a chef's book that people should be careful of anything that's prepared 'blackened,' because it's probably a ruse to cover up less-than-perfect ingredients. I disagree. I actually like the complex flavors of the spices here. This is a popular dish, and not just for our dieting customers." — Jeffrey Bleaken, Philadelphia Palm chef

¾ cup chicken stock, preferably homemade
¾ cup Jeffrey's Blackening Spice (page 78), or
  Paul Prudhomme's Magic Seasoning blend
8 boneless, skinless chicken breasts (5 to 6
  ounces each), patted dry with paper towels

⅓ cup canola oil
4 (¼-inch) lemon slices, for garnish
1½ tablespoons finely chopped flat-leaf parsley,
  for garnish

Preheat the oven to 400°. Pour the chicken stock into a large, ovenproof sauté pan, and place in the oven to heat.

Spread the Blackening Spice on a plate, and dredge both sides of each chicken breast in the spice, coating all the pieces as completely as possible. Place a large cast iron skillet over medium-high heat, and when it is very hot, add the oil. Sear the chicken for about 1½ minutes without moving, until dark golden brown but not burned; then turn and sear for 2 minutes more. Transfer the chicken breasts to the pan of stock in the oven, and finish cooking for 4 minutes, without turning.

Place two chicken breasts on each plate in a V formation. Quickly dip both sides of each lemon slice into the chopped parsley, and place one on the base of each V. Scatter a little more parsley around the edges of the plates, and serve immediately.

THAI-STYLE CHICKEN WITH FISH SAUCE AND BAMBOO SHOOTS

— SERVES 4 —

Washington, D.C., chef Sang Ek, a native of Cambodia, has been with the Palm for more than twenty-five years, and his contribution is acknowledged and

respected throughout the company. For a restaurant that takes decades to add a new dish to the menu, it is a testament to Sang's talent that he has contributed so many new ideas. Thai basil has a distinct flavor. Use it if you can find it or even better, use purple basil.

⅓ cup canola or other vegetable oil

4 cloves garlic, smashed with the side of a large, heavy knife and very finely chopped

1½ pounds boneless, skinless chicken breast, sliced ⅜ inch thick crosswise

¼ cup red chile paste with holy basil leaves (see Note)

¼ cup Thai fish sauce (see Note)

1 tablespoon sugar

8-ounce can bamboo shoots, drained well and cut into fine julienne

1 red bell pepper, cored, seeded, and cut into ¼-inch julienne

2 jalapeño peppers, cored, seeded, and thinly sliced

40 Thai basil leaves or, if available, purple basil

4 cups cooked white rice, for serving

Place a large sauté pan over high heat, and add the oil. When the oil is hot, add the garlic and stir constantly for 1 minute, until golden and aromatic. Add the sliced chicken breast, and stir-fry for 3 minutes, until firm, but still slightly pink in the center. Add the red chile paste, fish sauce, and sugar, and reduce the heat to medium-high. Cook, stirring occasionally, for about 5 minutes to blend the flavors. Stir in the bamboo shoots, red pepper, and jalapeño, and cook for 3 minutes more. Stir in the basil, and serve over white rice.

Note: Red chile paste with holy basil leaves and Thai fish sauce are available in well-stocked Asian markets.

CHICKEN CITRON

— SERVES 4 —

"There's pounding, and there's pounding. This isn't like veal scaloppini, where you gotta make the thing the size of a napkin and almost as thin. For Chicken Citron, you're just sort of evening the playing field." —Tony Tammero, executive chef

6 boneless, skinless chicken breasts (5 to 6 ounces each), trimmed of any ragged edges

Fine sea salt and freshly ground black pepper

2 large eggs

1 cup all-purpose flour, for dredging

1 cup seasoned dry Italian breadcrumbs,
   for dredging

¼ cup olive oil

3 tablespoons unsalted butter, at room
   temperature

1 large lemon, halved and juiced
   (reserve the juiced lemon halves)

Additional lemon juice, if needed,
   to make ⅓ cup

½ cup dry white wine

2 teaspoons very finely chopped flat-leaf parsley

½ lemon, cut into 4 wedges, for serving

Place each chicken breast between 2 sheets of plastic wrap on a work surface, and pound lightly, just to achieve an even thickness. This should only require 2 or 3 hits of the meat mallet for each breast. Remove the plastic wrap, and salt and pepper both sides of the chicken generously. In a large, shallow bowl, beat the eggs. Place the flour and breadcrumbs in two similar bowls, and set all three bowls near the stove.

Preheat the oven to 400°, and place a rimmed baking sheet inside to heat.

Dredge each breast first in the flour, shaking off the excess, and then the beaten egg, making sure it is completely coated and letting any excess drain back into the bowl. Finally, lay each piece on the breadcrumbs, pressing down first one side and then the other to firmly adhere the crumbs to the egg batter. Season both sides of the breaded breasts again with salt and pepper.

Place a large sauté pan over medium heat, and add the olive oil. When the oil is hot, add the chicken breasts without crowding (use two pans if necessary) and cook on one side until pale golden brown, about 2 minutes. Carefully turn and cook until pale golden, about 2 minutes more. Blot gently with paper towels to absorb excess oil, and transfer the breasts to the baking pan in the oven. Bake for 10 minutes, until the meat is firm and no trace of pink remains (if you like, use a meat thermometer and check that the temperature at the center has reached 160°).

While the breasts are baking, wipe out the sauté pan with paper towels and return to medium-high heat. Add 1 tablespoon of the butter and, when it is sizzling, add ⅓ cup lemon juice and the lemon halves. Add the white wine, ¼ teaspoon salt, and a few grindings of black pepper. When the liquid is simmering briskly, let it reduce for 2 minutes more; then remove the pan from the heat and add the remaining 2 tablespoons of butter. Shake the pan vigorously to emulsify the sauce. Transfer 2 breasts to each plate, and spoon a little of the sauce over the top. Scatter the parsley over the chicken and the edges of the plate, place a lemon wedge on the side of each, and serve at once.

Such is the American fascination with La Cosa Nostra that every successful Italian-run business is fodder for speculation. Connected? Who knows? All I know is that during the New York City garbage strike of 1993, the Palm was one of very few businesses that had their trash collected.

CHICKEN NEW ORLEANS

— SERVES 6 —

Chef Jeffrey Bleaken inhabits a kitchen in the Philadelphia Palm that is way too small for his talents. This dish, his personal contribution, made its debut as a lunch special. If you ever see Chicken New Orleans on a Palm menu, or hear it on a specials list, order it. In the meantime, cook it at home. This is one of those dishes that is far more than the sum of its parts. Don't know quite what to make of the combination of chicken and scallops? Trust me.

2 cups all-purpose flour, for dredging
Fine sea salt and freshly ground black pepper
1½ pounds boneless, skinless chicken breasts,
    cut into 1-inch cubes
2 tablespoons unsalted butter
1 pound large sea scallops, patted dry with
    paper towels
1½ teaspoons Cajun spice blend or
    best-quality chile powder

1 cup dry white wine
¾ cup chicken stock, preferably homemade
6 tablespoons unsalted butter, cut into 6 pieces,
    at room temperature
6 cups hot, cooked white or Creole-style rice,
    for serving
4 green onions, green parts only, coarsely
    chopped, for garnish

Place the flour on a large plate, and season it generously with salt and pepper. Pat the chicken cubes dry with paper towels. Warm six plates or large, shallow bowls in a low oven.

    Place a large sauté pan over high heat, and add the butter. When the butter foams, add the chicken and sauté, turning only occasionally, until firm and no longer pink on the outside (but not browned), about 2 minutes. Add the scallops, and sauté until they are no longer opaque, about 3 minutes more. Add the Cajun spice blend, and cook for 1 minute to release the flavor. Add the wine, and bring the mixture to a simmer. Cook, stirring occasionally, until the liquid is reduced by about three-quarters, 3 to 4 minutes. Add the chicken stock, and simmer until reduced by half, about 5 minutes more. Remove from the heat, and add the butter all at once, shaking the pan vigorously to emulsify the sauce. Spoon a portion of rice onto each warm plate, and top with generous spoonfuls of the chicken mixture. Scatter a little chopped green onion over each plate, and serve at once.

"Nobody's going to give you anything. You have to give it out of your heart because you want to. Being a general manager is a seven-day job. You don't go out, because there's always something to do. They tell you it's your restaurant, and yes, it is. But you gotta treat the guys right, because otherwise your restaurant won't run right. I been in L.A. since '76—some of my guys been here the whole time. You think you see that in other restaurants? No chance. The guys in the kitchen, [at] other restaurants the management sees them as the enemy. Lemme tell you, they're not the enemy. They're your life's blood."

—*Gigi Delmaestro, late L.A. Palm manager and Palm original*

CURRIED CHICKEN WITH CRISPY ALMONDS OVER BABY SPINACH

— SERVES 4 —

Washington, D.C., Palm chef Sang Ek has tried every curry powder there is. Since many of his friends are from the Caribbean, there was a bit of pressure for him to state a preference for Trinidadian and/or Jamaican curry. Sang will admit that his friend Steve's mom, who is from Trinidad, makes the best roti ever. But when it comes to this luscious sauce, he prefers Madras curry powder from India. Ideally, he'll soak up the curry sauce with a few of Steve's mom's rotis and call it heaven. This sauce may be made the night before, if desired.

CURRY SAUCE:

½ cup Madras curry powder (see Note)
½ cup water
¼ cup canola or other vegetable oil

3 cloves garlic, crushed with the side of a large, heavy knife and minced
1 small yellow onion, coarsely chopped

¼ cup soy sauce

1 cup canned coconut milk

1 tablespoon Thai green curry paste (see Note)

2 teaspoons olive oil

½ cup sliced almonds

Fine sea salt

⅓ cup canola or other vegetable oil

2 pounds boneless, skinless chicken breasts, sliced ⅜ inch thick across the grain

½ red bell pepper, seeded and cut into ¼-inch dice

1 tablespoon light brown sugar

1 stalk lemongrass, pale inner heart only, cut into 2-inch lengths

2 large jalapeño peppers, stemmed, seeded, and very finely diced

4 large cloves garlic, smashed with the side of a large, heavy knife and minced

1 cup dry white wine

2 pounds baby spinach leaves, well washed and dried

4 cups hot, cooked white rice, for serving

To make the Curry Sauce:

In a measuring cup, whisk the curry powder with the water and set aside.

Place a small saucepan over medium heat, and add the oil. When the oil is hot, add the garlic and onion; cook, stirring, for 3 to 4 minutes, until softened. Stir in the curry mixture and cook, stirring, until the mixture is almost dry, about 5 minutes. Add the soy sauce, coconut milk, curry paste, brown sugar, and lemongrass. Reduce the heat to a gentle simmer, and cook, stirring to break up the lumps, for about 10 minutes, until the consistency of heavy cream. Press the sauce through a fine strainer into a bowl; set aside, discarding the solids after pressing them firmly to extract as much flavor as possible.

To finish the dish: Place a small skillet over medium-high heat, and add the olive oil. Add the almonds and a pinch of salt, and cook for 3 minutes, shaking the pan occasionally, until golden brown. Drain the almonds on paper towels, and set aside.

Place a large sauté pan over high heat, and add the canola oil. When the oil is hot, add the chicken and stir-fry for 3 minutes, until firm and white but not cooked all the way through. Add the red peppers, jalapeño, and garlic and cook, stirring frequently, for about 3 minutes, until softened. Add the wine and simmer briskly for about 3 minutes, until slightly reduced. Stir in the reserved curry sauce, and simmer for 3 minutes more, until the sauce again reaches the consistency of heavy cream. Keep the chicken warm over very low heat, covered, while you cook the spinach.

Bring a generous amount of lightly salted water to a boil in a large saucepan. Add the spinach leaves all at once, and press down to submerge them completely. Cook for 1 minute and 15 seconds; then immediately drain in a colander. Press down firmly with the back of a large spoon to squeeze out as much water as possible. Using tongs, make a small mound of spinach in the center of each of 4 heated plates. Spoon the curried chicken on top, and sprinkle with the almonds. Serve the rice on the side.

Note: Madras curry powder and Thai green curry paste are available in well-stocked supermarkets or in Thai and Asian markets.

BROILED SPLIT CHICKEN

— SERVES 1 TO 3 —

This dish is tricky, but certainly do-able, using a home broiler. Since broilers vary in strength, keep an eye on the chicken and don't leave the kitchen while it's broiling. Rotate the pan if you see hot spots forming—on the breast, for instance— and if your broiler heating element is in the center, place the legs directly underneath it, with the breast closer to the edge of the oven, where it doesn't receive the full blast of heat. Once you've put the chicken in to bake, it's safe to tend to other business.

1 (2½- to 3-pound) chicken, preferably free-range	Fine sea salt and freshly ground black pepper
¼ cup olive oil	1 tablespoon finely chopped flat-leaf parsley, for serving

Rinse the chicken inside and out under cool running water, and pat dry thoroughly with paper towels. Let stand for 30 minutes at room temperature.

Preheat the broiler to high heat; if you have a separate oven, preheat it to 350°.

Split the chicken on either side of the backbone with poultry shears. Open the chicken out, breast side up, and press down to break a few of the rib bones and flatten the chicken slightly. With the skin side up, remove the wishbone with a small, sharp knife. With the skin side down, use your fingers and a knife to loosen the edges of the white, beak-shaped cartilage that extends from the bottom of the breastbone, and pull it free. Brush both sides of the chicken with the olive oil, and season generously with salt and pepper. Place the chicken skin side up, with knees together, on a flat rack set inside a broiler pan. Broil about 6 inches from the heat, with the door slightly ajar, for 8 minutes, until golden brown. Turn and broil the other side until golden, about 6 minutes more. Transfer the pan to the preheated oven or, if your broiler and oven are combined, turn off the broiler and set the oven to 350°. Roast for 5 minutes; then turn skin side up again and roast for 15 minutes more, until the juices at the thigh joint run clear. Tent the chicken loosely with foil, and let stand for 5 minutes; then serve whole for one person, or cut into smaller pieces through the joints to serve 2 or 3. Scatter the parsley over the chicken, and serve.

The Palm's aged New York strip steak needs no accompaniment—except perhaps a Michael Cope martini.

An order of double-cut Maryland lamb chops, a side of Asparagus Fritti—and to sip, a McClure Cocktail

A true Palm original, for the pasta course or as an entrée:
Linguine with Mortadella and Arugula à la Tony

Quality ingredients and Palm technique enhance Buffalo Mozzarella
with Tomatoes, Basil, and Extra-Virgin Olive Oil.

Seafood linguine prepared two ways: in White Clam Sauce fragrant with garlic, or with Clams and Shrimp Posillipo

Simple pleasures: the Palm's prime rib cut, USDA Prime, with a perfect Baked Potato and California cabernet.

"Don't let anyone tell you that large lobsters are tough," says Tony Tammero. The Palm is famous for massive ones.

Veal Malfata is not on any Palm menu. Arugula salad is a fabulous foil for the savory pounded veal rib chop.

*The Palm's crab cakes—served with Mango Salsa—are just briefly baked,
so the crabmeat stays nice and moist.*

*The first Palm, owned by two recent immigrants from Parma,
opened on New York City's Second Avenue in 1926.*

Veal Milanese is a sublime expression of the old way with veal; Spinach Aglio e Olio has been on the menu for decades.

Customers adore tender String Beans Marinara, and the "Half and Half" mix of Cottage Fries plus Fried Onions.

Use up leftover steak in Open-Faced Filet Mignon Sandwich
with Roasted Peppers, Fried Eggplant, and Fontina.

In 1973, a customer asked for "shrimps with garlic, but not broiled,"
and Jumbo Shrimp Sauté was the result.

"I looked up to see a guy sitting at the bar with a martini," recalls Tony Tammero.
That's how Veal Martini got its name.

Roasted Red Peppers and Anchovies is a steakhouse tradition with
a savory Palm twist, a recipe that dates to the 1950s.

In a "West Coast Gigi," hard-boiled egg and avocado enhance the venerable Gigi Salad, a longtime Palm favorite.

The Staples Center Palm in Los Angeles, opened in 2002, has the enduring charm of the original Second Avenue Palm.

Clams Bianco (in foreground, steamed with white wine, garlic, and basil), Clams Casino and Clams Oreganato

*The huge portion of New York Cheesecake, on the menu since 1965,
is meant to be shared among dinner partners.*

*Summer Pudding (foreground) and the Palm's signature Tiramisu,
a recipe developed after much experimentation*

CHICKEN MEDICI

— SERVES 2 —

"I found this recipe in a book many years ago, before I came to the Palm. It was actually called Chicken Bolognese. I ran it as a special a couple of times, and the waiters kept whining 'Where's the red sauce? Where's the meat sauce?' So I had to change the name. There was one group of guys who ate at the Palm frequently, and they just raved about this dish. That's when I put it on the menu. It has so many different elements: the sweetness of the marsala, the saltiness of the prosciutto, and the sharpness of the cheese—it's all over your tongue. Use plenty of marsala, because that's what creates the sauce. If you cook it a little too long and the pan is suddenly dry, just add a little more marsala and swirl the sauce back together. This very basic sauce is simply butter and wine, with a little flour to keep it together." —Jeffrey Bleaken, Philadelphia Palm chef

Once pounded out, these chicken breasts are too big to fit more than two in one pan without severe crowding. If you would like to double the recipe to serve 4, cook them in batches, or use two large skillets.

1 (10- to 12-ounce) whole boneless, skinless chicken breast, split down the center, with center cartilage removed
2 long, thin slices prosciutto, trimmed of fat and halved
½ cup all-purpose flour, for dredging
½ cup olive oil

⅔ cup marsala, preferably Florio
Fine sea salt and freshly ground black pepper
1 teaspoon chopped fresh sage
1 tablespoon unsalted butter, at room temperature
2 teaspoons freshly grated Parmigiano-Reggiano

Place each breast half on a work surface and, using a sharp knife, halve by cutting carefully from one side to the other, keeping both top and bottom pieces the same thickness. You should have a total of 4 thin medallions, the same size and shape as the original single breast but half as thick. Place each medallion between 2 sheets of plastic wrap on a work surface, and pound lightly, beginning in the center, to an even thickness of about ¼ inch. Remove the top sheet of plastic wrap from each chicken piece, and season with pepper. Trim the prosciutto slices to the same approximate size as the medallions, and place a trimmed slice on top of each medallion, matching up the edges. Replace the plastic wrap. Pound again briefly to flatten the medallions a little more and anchor the prosciutto securely on the top.

Preheat a broiler to medium-high heat, and place the oven rack and a broiler pan or rimmed baking sheet about 5 inches from the heat source.

On a plate, spread a generous amount of flour for dredging. Place a 12-inch, ovenproof sauté pan over medium-high heat. Dredge each chicken piece carefully in the flour, holding the prosciutto in place and shaking off the excess flour. Add the olive oil to the pan; when the oil is hot, sauté the chicken with the prosciutto side down until golden brown, about 1½ minutes, and then turn and cook until golden on the other side, 1½ minutes more. Remove from the heat and, holding the chicken in place with a spatula or tongs, tilt the pan to one side and spoon off the excess oil. Return to the heat, add the marsala, and simmer until reduced by about half and slightly thickened. Taste for seasoning, and correct with salt and pepper, if necessary (the prosciutto is salty, so go easy). Add the sage and butter, and shake the pan vigorously to emulsify the sauce. Transfer the chicken to the broiler pan, and scatter ½ teaspoon of Parmigiano over the top. Broil for about 1 minute, until the cheese is golden; then transfer to warmed plates and serve at once, spooning the pan sauce generously over the top.

Grilled Chicken and Roasted Red Pepper Sandwich

— Serves 4 —

This is a delicious dish—not just any old sandwich. Tony's variations on it include adding prosciutto and a few slices of provolone, which are melted briefly under the broiler. Try them both.

3 cloves garlic, finely chopped

1 large shallot, finely chopped

½ cup olive oil

Fine sea salt and freshly ground black pepper

4 boneless, skinless chicken breasts
  (5 to 6 ounces each)

¼ cup Pesto (recipe follows)

4 (8-inch) lengths French baguette,
  split horizontally

2 whole Roasted Red Peppers (page 182),
  or fire-roasted peppers in a jar

8 large basil leaves

16 baby arugula leaves, washed and dried

1 large ripe tomato, sliced paper-thin with
  a very sharp knife

Cottage Fries (page 170) (optional),
  for serving

In a shallow baking dish, combine the garlic, shallot, olive oil, ½ teaspoon salt, and ¼ teaspoon pepper. Whisk with a fork, and add the chicken breasts. Turn to coat them evenly, and cover with plastic wrap. Place in the refrigerator to marinate for 2 hours, turning once.

Preheat an indoor or outdoor grill to medium-high heat. Remove the chicken breasts from the refrigerator, and let them come to room temperature for 20 minutes. Grill for 4 to 5 minutes on each side, until the meat is firm and no longer pink in the center. Transfer to a cutting board, and let stand for about 5 minutes. Brush both sides of each breast with a little Pesto, and slice each one across the grain, ⅛ inch thick, on the diagonal.

Open each baguette length and brush the insides very lightly with Pesto. Place an equal amount of sliced chicken and half a roasted pepper on the base of each sandwich. Top each with 2 basil leaves, 4 arugula leaves, and 2 tomato slices, arranging all the ingredients evenly. Replace the top of the roll, and press down gently on the sandwiches. Serve with Cottage Fries, if desired.

Pesto

2 cups firmly packed basil leaves
2 cloves garlic, finely chopped
2 tablespoons pine nuts, lightly toasted

Fine sea salt and freshly ground black pepper
½ cup olive oil
½ cup freshly grated Parmigiano-Reggiano

In a food processor, combine the basil, garlic, pine nuts, ½ teaspoon salt, and ¼ teaspoon pepper. Process, scraping down the sides of the bowl, until the mixture is pureed. With the motor running, add the olive oil slowly, in a thin stream. Transfer the mixture to a bowl, and stir in the Parmigiano. Use immediately, or keep refrigerated in an airtight container and use within 2 days.

VEAL DEMIGLACE

— YIELD: ABOUT 2 QUARTS —

This versatile reduced stock acts as a building block to great sauces and braises, but it is not an ingredient that can be used alone. It will keep in an airtight container for up to a week in the refrigerator and for three to six months in the freezer. Freeze in 1- or 2-cup quantities for extra convenience.

10 pounds veal knuckle bones

4 medium carrots, washed and cut into
   1-inch pieces

2 large onions, quartered, with skins left on

½ cup tomato paste

1 cup dry white wine

Preheat the oven to 400°. In a large roasting pan, roast the veal bones for 1½ hours, turning them every 30 minutes. Add the carrots and onions, stir, and roast for 45 minutes more, until the bones and vegetables are nicely browned. Stir in the tomato paste, and roast for 5 minutes more; then transfer all the ingredients to a large stockpot. Pour off and discard the excess fat from the roasting pan, and set the pan over medium-low heat. Add the wine and 2 cups water to the pan, and deglaze it, stirring and scraping the bottom and sides to release all the flavorful bits. Pour the deglazing liquid over the bones and vegetables in the stockpot, and add enough water to cover the ingredients by about 4 inches. Bring to a simmer over medium-low heat; then reduce the heat to low. Simmer very gently, uncovered, for 7 to 8 hours. Occasionally, skim off any impurities that rise to the surface, and when the water falls below the top of the ingredients, add a bit more. At the end of the cooking time, the ingredients should still be covered by about 2 inches of liquid. Strain the stock through a colander lined with a double thickness of slightly dampened cheesecloth, pressing down hard on the solids to extract all their flavor. Discard the solids. In a large, clean saucepan, simmer the liquid over medium-high heat until it has reduced to about two-thirds of its original volume.

— CHAPTER 6 —

Pasta

LINGUINE WITH WHITE CLAM SAUCE

— SERVES 4 —

Wally Ganzi and Tony Tammero made this dish when they appeared on Dinah Shore's television show.

One often overlooked but crucial secret to serving great pasta is to warm the serving bowl and plates. Pasta cools quickly once it leaves the hot pan, and heaping it onto cold plates compounds the damage.

3½ cups shucked clams, preferably from
    eastern waters, with all their juices
    (about 3 dozen)
Kosher salt, for cooking the pasta
¼ cup olive oil
5 medium cloves garlic, crushed with the side
    of a large, heavy knife
¼ teaspoon red pepper flakes, or to taste

½ cup dry white wine
1 pound imported dried linguine,
    preferably DeCecco
½ cup chicken stock
Fine sea salt and freshly ground black pepper,
    for seasoning
1 tablespoon unsalted butter
¾ cup julienne of fresh basil, loosely packed

Pick over the clams, and remove any bits of shell. Coarsely chop the clams, and set them aside. Strain all the juices through a fine strainer to remove any grit or sand. Put a large pot of well-salted water on to boil for the pasta. Place a large serving bowl and 4 pasta bowls in a low oven to warm.

In a large sauté pan, heat the olive oil over medium-low heat, and add the garlic and pepper flakes. Stir constantly until just golden brown, but do not let the garlic burn. Add the clams and their juices, increase the heat to medium-high, and toss for 30 seconds. Add the white wine, and simmer until reduced by a quarter, about 5 minutes.

At this point, the water for the pasta should be boiling furiously. Add the pasta and stir; after a few minutes, reduce the heat slightly to prevent the water from boiling over. Cook until al dente, about 10 minutes. To the clam mixture, add the chicken stock, ½ teaspoon salt, and 4 turns of the peppermill, or to taste. Cook rapidly until the sauce is reduced by one-third and is slightly thickened, about 5 minutes. If desired, remove the garlic.

Drain the pasta thoroughly, and return it to the pot in which it was cooked. Add the butter, and toss well. Transfer a little of the sauce to the warmed serving bowl, and add the pasta and the basil. Toss and serve at once, mounding the lightly dressed pasta into the warm bowls and topping each with an equal portion of the clams and remaining sauce.

At first glance, the portion sizes in this chapter may seem meager when compared with the usual Palm-sized servings. Remember, Italians eat a pasta course before their main course, so 4 ounces of dried pasta per person is plenty when followed by Veal Parmigiana or Steak à La Stone. If you plan to dine American style, with pasta as your main course, double all the ingredients in these recipes except the salt—increase the amount of salt by only about 25 percent, rather than by half.

LINGUINE WITH RED CLAM SAUCE

— SERVES 4 —

In the restaurant world, this kind of cooking is often referred to as "a la minute," which means cooked to order. Happily, that also makes such simple dishes easy for the home cook to re-create. If you measure and chop all the ingredients and start cooking them before you put the linguine in the water, this is literally made while the pasta cooks. If the juice in the canned tomatoes is watery, drain them slightly, but if it's quite thick, add a few tablespoons to the pan.

3½ cups shucked clams, preferably from eastern waters, with all their juices (about 3 dozen)
Kosher salt, for cooking the pasta
¼ cup olive oil
5 cloves garlic, crushed with the side of a large, heavy knife
¼ teaspoon red pepper flakes (or to taste)
½ cup dry white wine

1 pound imported dried linguine, preferably DeCecco
½ cup chicken stock
1½ cups canned Italian plum tomatoes (about 6), drained and coarsely chopped
Fine sea salt and freshly ground black pepper
¾ cup julienne of fresh basil, loosely packed
1 tablespoon unsalted butter

Pick over the clams, and remove any bits of shell. Coarsely chop the clams, and place in a strainer over a bowl, reserving all the juices. Put a large pot of well-salted water on to boil for the pasta. Place a large serving bowl and 4 pasta bowls in a low oven to warm.

In a large sauté pan, heat the olive oil over medium-low heat, and add the garlic and pepper flakes. Stir constantly until just golden brown—do not let the garlic burn. Add the clams and their juices, increase the heat to medium-high, and toss for 30 seconds. Add the white wine, and simmer until reduced by a quarter, about 5 minutes.

At this point, the pasta water should be boiling furiously. Add the pasta and stir; after a few minutes, reduce the heat slightly to prevent the water from boiling over. Cook until al dente, about 10 minutes. To the clam mixture, add the chicken stock, tomatoes, ½ teaspoon salt, and 12 turns of the peppermill, or to taste. Cook rapidly until the sauce is reduced by a third and slightly thickened. If desired, remove the garlic.

Drain the pasta thoroughly, and return it to the pot in which it was cooked. Add the butter, and toss thoroughly. Transfer a little of the sauce to the warmed serving bowl, and add the pasta and basil. Toss together and serve at once, mounding the lightly dressed pasta in the warm bowls and topping with an equal portion of the clams and remaining sauce.

Try to use canned Italian plum tomatoes, preferably San Marzanos. If you do, crushing them with one hand as you add them to the pan will be preparation enough. If only California tomatoes are available, you'll have to cut out the hard core, and if they're too tough to crush by hand, you may need to chop them. Good Italian plum tomatoes rarely require sugar to balance acidity in a sauce, but California tomatoes are so tart that you'll probably find the addition of ½ teaspoon sugar per 28-ounce can a good idea.

LINGUINE WITH MORTADELLA AND ARUGULA À LA TONY

— SERVES 2 —

The mortadella for this unusual but very simple dish must be torn by hand. Slicing or cutting just won't do, says Tony. He prefers to use pure olive oil for cooking the garlic in this recipe, because he feels the peppery extra-virgin oil might overwhelm the delicate flavor of the mortadella. But a discreet dash of it at the end adds a nice little zing. This is another of those indispensable "while the pasta cooks" recipes, so be sure to do your preparation and measuring before you put the pasta into the boiling water. Note that this dish doesn't appear on any Palm menu, because Tony feels he's the only chef who can make it properly.

Kosher salt, for cooking the pasta
½ pound dried imported linguine, preferably
  DeCecco
¼ cup olive oil
2 large cloves garlic, crushed with the side
  of a large, heavy knife
½ pound thinly sliced mortadella, torn into
  2- to 3-inch pieces

1 pound baby arugula, stemmed, washed,
  and dried
⅛ teaspoon crushed red pepper flakes,
  or to taste
Fine sea salt and freshly ground black pepper
¼ cup chicken or vegetable stock
Extra virgin olive oil, for drizzling

Place all the ingredients near the stove, and place 2 large pasta bowls or plates in a low oven to warm.

Put a large pot of lightly salted water on to boil for the pasta. When the water is boiling furiously, add the pasta and stir; after a few minutes, reduce the heat slightly to prevent the water from boiling over. Cook until al dente, about 10 minutes.

As soon as you add the pasta to the pot, place a large sauté pan over medium heat and add the olive oil. When the pan is hot, add the garlic. Cook, stirring, for about 2 minutes, until the garlic is just golden brown; do not let it burn. Add the mortadella, and sauté for 2½ to 3 minutes, until aromatic and golden around the edges. Add the arugula, crushed red pepper, ½ teaspoon salt, and 2 turns of the peppermill, and toss over the heat for 1 minute more. The arugula should be just slightly wilted. Remove the pan from the heat.

Drain the pasta, reserving about 1 tablespoon of the cooking water, and return the pasta to the pot in which it was cooked. Add the chicken stock, the mortadella mixture, and the reserved pasta water. Toss together and serve at once, mounding the pasta into the warm bowls and distributing the ingredients equally. Remove the garlic, if desired. Drizzle each portion with a little extra-virgin olive oil, and serve at once.

"In Dominic's day, the Palm had the original 'open kitchen.' It was so open, you could practically cook your food from the bar. Of course, if you didn't know Bruno Molinari, the manager, you'd never get a table anyway."

—Eddie Byrne, *Palm Too assistant general manager*

Spaghetti Marinara

Marinara sauce is one of the crucial building blocks of southern Italian cooking, and despite the fact that the restaurant's cooking is northern Italian in origin, marinara is equally important at the Palm. There, the simple goodness of this time-honored sauce complements a bowl of al dente pasta, sits alongside a plateful of crisp-fried Calamari Fritti, and luxuriously coats green beans redolent with garlic. With such a deceptively simple sauce, the quality of your ingredients is paramount. Be sure to use Italian plum tomatoes—if possible, from San Marzano.

Kosher salt, for cooking the pasta
1¼ pounds dried imported spaghetti,
  preferably DeCecco

2 cups Marinara Sauce (recipe follows)
6 large leaves fresh basil, torn into small pieces

Put a large pot of generously salted water on to boil for the pasta. Place 4 or 6 pasta bowls in a low oven to warm.

In a small saucepan, warm the Marinara Sauce over medium heat.

When the water is boiling furiously, add the pasta and stir; after a few minutes, reduce the heat slightly to prevent the water from boiling over. Cook until al dente, about 10 minutes. A few minutes before the pasta is done, pour half of the marinara sauce into a large sauté pan and place over medium heat. Drain the pasta thoroughly, and add to the sauce. Toss with tongs to coat with the marinara. Transfer the pasta to warm bowls, and spoon some of the remaining sauce on top. Scatter with the basil, and serve at once.

Marinara Sauce
YIELD: 4 CUPS

This is a very quick, light sauce—in Palermo it's called "fry-pan sauce." Taste your tomatoes before using them. If they're mild and sweet, you won't need to add any sugar. However, if they're too acidic, add about 1 teaspoon sugar. Tomatoes also vary in meatiness, and there is no way to know how thick the sauce will be until it's finished. For topping pasta, a thin sauce is fine, but if you will be using the marinara for a baked dish such as Veal Parmigiana, or a sauteed dish like String

Beans Marinara, you want a sauce that coats the back of a spoon. To thicken it slightly, use your fingertips (so you can feel when all the starch has dissolved) to mix 1½ to 2 teaspoons of cornstarch with 3 tablespoons water, and stir into the sauce 10 minutes after adding the wine.

¼ cup olive oil
6 cloves garlic, crushed with the side of
  a large, heavy knife
2 (28-ounce) cans Italian plum tomatoes,
  with juice

½ cup dry white wine
Fine sea salt and freshly ground black pepper
¼ teaspoon crushed red pepper flakes
½ cup fresh basil leaves, loosely packed

Place a large sauté pan over medium-high heat, and add the olive oil. Add the garlic and sauté, stirring, until golden, about 2 minutes. Do not allow the garlic to burn. Add the tomatoes, crushing them thoroughly with your hand, along with their juice, and stir. Bring to a boil, uncovered; then reduce the heat so that the sauce simmers gently. Add the wine, 1 teaspoon salt, a few turns of the peppermill, and the red pepper. Simmer for 20 minutes, stirring occasionally. The sauce will be fairly thin. Stir in the basil, and remove from the heat. The sauce may be cooled to room temperature and refrigerated for up to 4 days or frozen in small quantities for up to 1 month. (In fact, the flavor will improve.) Remove the basil leaves and garlic before serving, if desired.

"When I first came to California to be a film actress there were many levels of success and different ways to attain it . . . I'd had ten years in the theatre in New York, and the audience there tells you who you are. But in Hollywood you don't hear applause. Wally Ganzi was one of the first ones to put my painting on the wall of his restaurant, and call me to say, 'Hey kiddo, you're a big star! Come on down, we need you here.'

"Hey, the guy was from New York city, they don't lie there.

"When I came to Hollywood years ago, we were all beautiful babies. We all wore white. We were all building a staircase to paradise, to the greatest success we could attain. We were all thin, hungry, and so ambitious—it was the seventies, we were beautiful, oh, so beautiful! And you'd walk in to the Palm restaurant and see your painting up on the wall—well, let's just put it this way: you learned to eat, and eat well, and make real friends and appreciate great dining and great conversation. We had a ball!

"Thanks for everything, Wally, I love you."

—Brenda Vaccaro, at the opening party for the Staples Center Palm in Downtown Los Angeles, 4/4/02.

SPAGHETTI CARBONARA

— SERVES 4 TO 6 —

Adding stock makes this fabulous pasta extra-creamy. It's a deceptively simple dish that is actually quite difficult to do well. You've probably had some mediocre versions, but this one could well become your "carbonara for life." In a pinch, 2 cups of the pasta cooking water, with all those good minerals and starch, can be substituted for the stock. Or for a really complex flavor, substitute Veal Demiglace (page 139) diluted by half with water. The Palm restaurants use Citerio brand pancetta.

Kosher salt, for cooking the pasta

2 cups light veal or chicken stock, or
    pasta cooking water

3 tablespoons olive oil

8 ounces pancetta, cut into ¼-inch dice

½ onion, finely chopped

4 cloves garlic, crushed with the side of
    a large, heavy knife

1¼ pounds dried imported spaghetti,
    preferably DeCecco

¾ cup freshly grated Parmigiano-Reggiano

¼ cup dry white wine

2 large egg yolks

2 tablespoons finely chopped flat-leaf parsley

Fine sea salt, for seasoning, if necessary

Freshly ground black pepper

Put a large pot of generously salted water on to boil for the pasta. In a small saucepan, warm the stock over very low heat. Place 4 to 6 pasta bowls in a low oven to warm. Assemble all the remaining ingredients near the stove.

Heat a large sauté pan over medium-low heat, and add the olive oil. Add the pancetta and cook, stirring occasionally, until crisp. Drain off and discard all but 2 tablespoons of fat from the pan. Add the onion, and stir for 1 minute; then add the garlic and cook, shaking the pan, for about 1½ minutes more, until golden brown. Do not let the garlic burn. Remove the pan from the heat, discard the garlic, and stir in 1 cup of the hot stock. Set at the back of the stove.

When the water is boiling furiously, add the pasta and stir; after a few minutes, reduce the heat slightly to prevent the water from boiling over. Cook until al dente, about 10 minutes. Drain the pasta thoroughly, and place the empty pot over very low heat. Add the Parmigiano, wine, egg yolks, and parsley, stirring quickly. Immediately add the well-drained pasta, and toss well with tongs to coat each strand. Add the pancetta-onion mixture, toss again, and add a little more of the hot stock, if desired, to make the sauce creamier. Taste for seasoning. If you use good Parmigiano and pancetta, the dish will probably not need additional salt. Serve at once in the warmed bowls, passing the peppermill at the table.

DOMINIC'S BEEF À LA DUTCH

— SERVES 2 AS A MAIN COURSE, OR 4 AS A PASTA COURSE —

"This is a real old-time dish from the '20s. We pan-sear filet mignons, then add onions and red peppers with brown stock. You finish it with a little fresh butter, and serve over pasta." —Tony Tammero, executive chef

Kosher salt, for cooking the pasta

4 filet mignon steaks (3 ounces each, about 2 inches thick), at room temperature

Fine sea salt and freshly ground black pepper

2 tablespoons olive oil

½ large white onion, diced

1 large clove garlic, crushed with the side of a large, heavy knife

2 green bell peppers, cored, seeded, and cut into ¼-inch matchsticks

2 bay leaves

½ cup marsala

½ cup Veal Demiglace (see Note)

1 pound dried imported fettucine, preferably DeCecco

1 tablespoon unsalted butter, at room temperature

Put a large pot of generously salted water on to boil for the pasta. Place 2 to 4 pasta bowls or plates in a low oven to warm.

Pat the steaks dry with paper towels, and season both sides generously with salt and pepper. Place a large sauté pan over high heat, and add the olive oil. When the oil is very hot but not smoking, add the steaks and reduce the heat to medium-high. Sear on each side for about 1½ minutes; you want a nice crust, so don't move the steaks until you are ready to turn them. Transfer to a plate and set aside. Pour off the excess oil from the pan, leaving a slight film. Return the pan to medium-low heat.

Add the onion, garlic, green pepper, and bay leaves to the pan, and cook, stirring occasionally, until the onions are almost translucent, about 10 minutes. Return the beef to the pan, and add the marsala and Veal Demiglace. Simmer slowly over very low heat, uncovered, for about 12 minutes for medium rare. As soon as the steaks are returned to the pan, add the fettucine to the boiling water and stir; after a few minutes, reduce the heat slightly to prevent the water from boiling over. Cook until al dente, about 10 minutes.

While the pasta and the steaks are cooking, turn the steaks over once or twice, spooning the sauce and vegetables over them to baste. The vegetables should be quite tender.

Drain the pasta thoroughly, and return it to the pot in which it was cooked. Add the butter and toss thoroughly. Add a few spoonfuls of the sauce and vegetables; toss, then transfer equal portions of pasta to each warm plate, discarding the garlic, if desired. Place 1 steak (or 2 steaks, if serving just 2 people) atop each portion of pasta, and spoon on the remaining sauce and vegetables, discarding the bay leaves. Serve at once.

Note: There are two sources for Veal Demiglace, which is made as a matter of course in all good restaurants:

   1. If you have time, you can make your own (page 139)—it will last for ages and make many, many dinners taste quite wonderful.

   2. Gourmet shops now sell small portions of demiglace (or to mail order, visit www.vatelcuisine.com).

SPAGHETTINI AGLIO E OLIO

— SERVES 4 —

Good olive oil, fresh and juicy garlic, and the best-quality imported pasta will spell success with this elemental dish. If you don't have any stock on hand, or just want a simpler flavor, reserve ½ cup of the pasta cooking water just before you drain it, and use in place of the stock.

Kosher salt, for cooking the pasta
½ cup chicken or veal stock
1 pound dried, imported spaghettini,
   preferably DeCecco
½ cup olive oil
8 large cloves garlic, smashed with the side
   of a large, heavy knife

3 whole leaves fresh basil, torn into halves,
   or quarters if large
Fine sea salt
1 tablespoon unsalted butter, at room
   temperature (optional)

Put a large pot of generously salted water on to boil. In a small saucepan, heat the stock and set at the back of the stove over very low heat. Place 4 pasta bowls in a low oven to warm.

   When the water is boiling vigorously, add the pasta and stir; after a few minutes, reduce the heat slightly to prevent the water from boiling over. Cook until al dente, about 10 minutes.

   Heat a large nonstick or cast iron skillet over medium heat, and add the olive oil. When the oil is hot, add the garlic and let it sizzle for 1 minute. Remove the pan from the heat, and let the garlic continue to cook in the residual heat. Turn the garlic to brown both sides.

   Return the pan of oil and garlic to very low heat, and add the basil. When the pasta is cooked, drain and add it, along with the warm stock, to the garlic and oil. Using tongs, toss the pasta gently but thoroughly (add the butter here, if desired, for additional richness). Add about ½ teaspoon salt, toss again, and serve at once in the warm bowls.

"When the oil's nice and hot, I throw in fresh basil leaves, so they almost deep-fry. They're crispy, and all the flavor is infused in the oil. I just crush the garlic. I never use chopped garlic, absolutely never. Chopped garlic becomes too pungent, and because you can't control the temperature of the oil, it could burn. I don't count the cloves; I weigh them —½ to 1 ounce for this dish. And I serve them in the pasta. Some people eat them, some don't. I always eat the garlic."

—*Tony Tammero, executive chef*

Rigatoni with Portobello Mushrooms and Goat Cheese

— Serves 6 —

This is certainly not a traditional Italian recipe, but it's very popular at Palm One in New York City. It's a great example of a contemporary American take on pasta that might not sit well with a classical Italian chef but that pushes all the right buttons with today's sophisticated palates.

"This pasta has a lot of flavor, and the goat cheese adds just the right amount of creaminess. To make it even more outstanding, grill or roast the portobello mushrooms after they have marinated for an hour. Marinate for 30 minutes to 1 hour; then grill or roast until tender and dry. Slice and proceed with the recipe."

— Brian McCardle, Palm One chef

Caramelized Onions:

2 tablespoons olive oil

*2 large portobello mushroom caps, brushed
clean with a soft, dry brush or paper towels*

1 large white onion, sliced paper-thin

*½ cup plus 2 tablespoons olive oil
Fine sea salt and freshly ground black pepper*

1 teaspoon chopped fresh thyme

1 teaspoon chopped fresh rosemary

Kosher salt, for cooking the pasta

1 small shallot, finely chopped

1 clove garlic, finely chopped

⅓ cup dry white wine

⅓ cup chicken stock

2 ounces soft, fresh goat cheese, such as
Montrachet

2 teaspoons unsalted butter, at room
temperature

6 large leaves fresh basil, cut into julienne

1½ pounds dried imported rigatoni, preferably
DeCecco

First, make the caramelized onions: place a sauté pan over medium-low heat, and add the olive oil. Add the onions, and sauté very slowly, stirring and turning occasionally, until golden brown, 45 minutes to 1 hour. Set aside, or cover and refrigerate until needed, up to 24 hours.

Trim the stems and use a spoon to scrape away the black gills from the underside of the mushrooms, to keep them from bleeding color while they marinate. In a bowl, cover the mushrooms with ½ cup of the olive oil, ½ teaspoon salt, a few turns of the peppermill, and the fresh herbs. Turn to coat, and marinate for 30 minutes to 1 hour, turning several times. Remove the mushrooms from the marinade, and slice them ¼ inch thick on the diagonal. Set aside.

Put a large pot of generously salted water on to boil for the pasta, and warm a large serving bowl and 6 pasta bowls or plates in a low oven.

Place a large sauté pan over medium heat, and add the remaining 2 tablespoons of olive oil. Add the shallots and garlic and cook, stirring, for 2 minutes. Add the caramelized onions and sliced mushrooms; sauté, stirring occasionally, until the mushrooms begin to release some of their liquid, about 5 minutes. Add the white wine and deglaze, simmering until reduced by half, about 3 minutes more. Add the chicken stock, and reduce again by half, about 3 minutes. Stir in the goat cheese, butter, and basil. Taste for seasoning and correct, if necessary. Remove the pan from the heat, and cover to keep warm while you cook the pasta.

When the water is boiling furiously, add the rigatoni and stir; after a few minutes, reduce the heat slightly to prevent the water from boiling over. Cook until al dente, about 10 minutes; then drain thoroughly and transfer to the warm serving bowl. Add half of the hot sauce to the pasta, and toss well. Transfer the pasta to the warmed bowls, and top each one with a large spoonful of the remaining sauce.

Maureen Dowd, in *The New York Times Magazine,* March 6, 1994, wrote about the caricatures in the Washington, D.C., Palm: " The Palm . . . will put up drawings of almost any good customer and leave them up. 'We do not really ax somebody just because they're out of favor,' says Tommy Jacomo, the Damon Runyon-esque maitre d'hotel and curator of the images. 'There are a lot of people on the wall, like Jacob Javits and Rogers Morton and stuff, that have been dead, and they just go on and on.' . . . The faces come at you in fast-forward."

"Gigi [Delmaestro] and I actually double-dated once—Italian twin sisters. My entire family—me, my father, my sister Penny—we were all on the wall at the West Hollywood Palm, and then they put a wine rack in front of us."

—*producer/director Garry Marshall*

RISOTTO MILANESE

— SERVES 6 —

If you use real Parmigiano-Reggiano, this simple, honest dish will probably not need additional salt. Domestic versions of generic Parmesan are generally not as salty. Be sure to taste, and decide, before serving. For a dish like this, it is worth making your own chicken stock, if possible.

½ teaspoon chopped saffron threads, or
 ¼ teaspoon powdered saffron
6 cups warm chicken stock, preferably
 homemade
3 tablespoons unsalted butter
2 tablespoons olive oil

1 medium onion, very finely chopped
2 cups Arborio or Carnaroli rice
Freshly ground black pepper
⅓ cup freshly grated Parmigiano-Reggiano,
 plus extra for serving
Fine sea salt, if necessary

In a small bowl, soak the saffron threads in 1 cup of the warm stock for 20 minutes.

Keep the remaining stock hot, but not boiling, in a small saucepan while you start cooking the risotto. In a large, heavy saucepan over medium-high heat, combine 1 tablespoon of the butter, the olive oil, and the onion. Stir until the onion is translucent, about 5 minutes. Add the rice, and stir to coat each grain with the oil and butter. Add ½ cup of the hot stock, and continue stirring until almost all of the liquid has been absorbed into the rice. Keep adding the stock, ½ cup at a time, stirring thoroughly and reaching your spoon into all edges of the pan. After about 9 minutes, add the saffron-infused stock. Total cooking time should be about 18 minutes to achieve the perfect consistency. When cooked properly, the rice should be firm to the bite and the mixture should be creamy. Remove from the heat, and stir in the remaining 2 tablespoons of butter, a few turns of the peppermill, and the Parmigiano. Stir until the cheese has melted. Taste for seasoning, and add a little salt, if necessary. Serve immediately, with extra grated Parmigiano on the side.

PENNE BOLOGNESE

— SERVES 6 —

This is a rich and unctuous version of the ragu known in the old Italian neighborhoods as "The Sauce." It might taste a little different from house to house and block to block, but it always started with similar ingredients. In some houses, it took twenty-four hours to make.

3 tablespoons olive oil
1 small white onion, finely chopped
1 medium carrot, finely chopped
1 rib celery, finely chopped
1 small clove garlic, finely chopped
2 to 3 bay leaves
5 ounces lean ground pork
5 ounces ground veal
5 ounces lean ground beef
1 cup full-bodied red wine

2 (28-ounce) cans peeled plum tomatoes, preferably Italian, with juice
1 cup heavy cream
Fine sea salt and freshly ground black pepper
½ cup grated Parmigiano-Reggiano
8 large leaves fresh basil, cut into julienne
Kosher salt, for cooking the pasta
1½ pounds dried imported penne, preferably DeCecco

Place a large, heavy pot over medium-low heat, and add the olive oil. Add the onion, carrot, and celery, and cook gently, stirring occasionally, for about 10 minutes, until the onions are translucent. Add the garlic and bay leaves, and cook for 1 minute. Add the pork, veal, and beef, and cook, stirring to break up any chunks, for about 7 minutes, until the beef is no longer pink. Add the wine, and increase the heat to high. Cook for about 5 minutes to reduce slightly. Add the plum tomatoes, crushing them with one hand as you add them to the pot, along with their juice. Add the cream, and reduce the heat to low. Cook for 1½ hours, uncovered, stirring every 10 minutes or so. Add ¾ teaspoon salt and 4 to 5 turns of the peppermill, and cook for 10 minutes more. Taste for seasoning, and stir in the Parmigiano and the basil.

Put a large pot of salted water over high heat for the pasta, and warm 6 pasta bowls in a low oven. When the water is boiling furiously, add the penne and stir; after a few minutes, reduce the heat slightly to prevent the water from boiling over. Cook until al dente, about 10 minutes; then drain thoroughly. Return the pasta to the pot in which it was cooked, and add about a quarter of the sauce. Toss to mix thoroughly, and transfer the pasta to the warm pasta bowls. Top each serving with large spoonfuls of the remaining sauce, and serve at once.

TONY'S MOM'S LASAGNA

— SERVES 10 TO 12, WITH ABUNDANT LEFTOVERS —

This dish is best prepared in stages. You'll need to drain the ricotta and shape the meatballs a day in advance. Note that the ricotta (which absolutely must be whole milk) should be drained overnight in the refrigerator, in a sieve set over a bowl. This prevents the lasagna from being watery and is an essential step for success. You will need a 12 x 20-inch baking pan that is 3 inches deep. If you only have a smaller pan, it must be deeper than 3 inches to accommodate all the layers.

MEATBALLS (SHAPE A DAY IN ADVANCE):

½ cup pine nuts

5 slices stale white bread, crusts removed (if bread is fresh, dry it for 30 minutes in a very low oven after removing the crust)

¼ pound lean (80/20) ground beef chuck

¼ pound ground pork

½ pound ground veal

1 clove garlic, crushed with the side of a large, heavy knife and finely chopped

½ cup loosely packed flat-leaf parsley leaves, chopped

Fine sea salt and freshly ground black pepper

1 large egg, lightly beaten

½ cup grated Parmigiano-Reggiano

In a small, dry skillet, toast the pine nuts for 1 to 2 minutes over medium heat, shaking the pan, until light golden and aromatic. Watch carefully, for they can burn in the blink of an eye. Place in a large bowl and set aside.

Place the bread in a small bowl, and cover with 1 cup warm water. Let stand for 10 minutes, turning to moisten evenly. Squeeze gently to remove some, but not all, of the water, and tear into 2-inch chunks. Add to the bowl with the pine nuts.

To the bread mixture, add the beef, pork, veal, garlic, parsley, 1 teaspoon salt, a generous quantity of black pepper, the egg, and the Parmigiano. Use your hands to combine the meatball ingredients thoroughly. Occasionally rinse your hands under warm running water to keep the fat from sticking to them.

Form the mixture into meatballs slightly larger than a golf ball, and place them on a baking sheet. You should have about 24 meatballs. Tent with plastic wrap, and refrigerate overnight.

SAUCE:

2 tablespoons olive oil

1½ pounds sweet Italian sausage

1½ pounds hot Italian sausage

1 (6-ounce) can tomato paste

¼ cup dry red wine, such as chianti

3 (28-ounce) cans Italian plum tomatoes, with juice

Fine sea salt and freshly ground black pepper

3 bay leaves

1 teaspoon sugar

Remove the meatballs from the refrigerator, and let them stand at room temperature for 30 minutes. Place a large nonstick sauté pan over medium heat. When it is hot, add the oil. Add the meatballs, in batches if necessary, and cook until golden on all sides, about 6 minutes. Do not try to turn or move the meatballs for 2 minutes after you first add them to the pan—they need time to "seize' so that they don't fall apart. With a slotted spoon, transfer the lightly browned meatballs to a platter lined with paper towels. Add the sausages to the same pan, and brown on all sides in the remaining oil, in batches if necessary, poking each one in several places with a fork to pierce the casing and let the fat run out. Cook for 7 minutes. The meatballs and sausage will be partially cooked at this point. Remove the sausages from the pan, and drain on paper towels.

In the same pan, add the tomato paste and cook over medium heat for 2 minutes, stirring with a wooden spoon. Add the red wine, and stir until smooth. Transfer the mixture to a large pot or Dutch oven, scraping out all the flavorful juices from the sauté pan. Add the tomatoes, crushing them with one hand, and all their juice, ¾ teaspoon salt, a generous grinding of black pepper, the bay leaves, and the sugar. Cook, stirring, for 6 to 7 minutes, until just beginning to simmer. Add the meatballs and sausage, pushing them down gently to submerge them in the sauce. Reduce the heat to very low, or use a "flame tamer" to prevent scorching. Cook the sauce, uncovered, for 2 hours. Occasionally, stir gently with a wooden spoon, taking care not to break up the meatballs too much. Taste for seasoning, and adjust with salt and pepper. Remove from the heat, and let stand at room temperature for 1 to 3 hours before assembling the lasagna. If desired, cool the sauce to room temperature and refrigerate it overnight before assembling and baking the lasagna. Return to room temperature before proceeding. Remove the bay leaves.

LASAGNA:

1 quart whole-milk ricotta, drained in a sieve
   overnight in the refrigerator
1 large egg yolk
¼ cup chopped flat-leaf parsley
2 cups grated Parmigiano-Reggiano or
   Pecorino-Romano

2 pounds dried imported lasagna noodles,
   preferably DeCecco
⅓ cup kosher salt
¼ cup plus 2 tablespoons olive oil
2 pounds sliced Muenster cheese, orange
   edges trimmed

In a large bowl, combine the ricotta, egg yolk, parsley, and ¼ cup of the Parmigiano. Mix thoroughly, and let stand at room temperature for 1 hour before assembling the lasagna. (If desired, mix ahead of time and refrigerate; then let stand at room temperature for 1 hour before using.)

Put a large pot of water on to boil. When it reaches a rolling boil, add the noodles, salt, and 2 tablespoons olive oil. Add the noodles one at a time, to prevent them from sticking together. Cook until al dente, no more than 7 minutes, gently turning and separating the noodles with a spatula. Drain in a colander, and shake very gently to drain the excess water. As soon as they are cool enough to handle (wearing clean rubber gloves if your hands are sensitive to heat), drizzle the noodles generously with ¼ cup olive oil, lifting and rearranging them gently with your hands so that each one is lightly coated. Transfer the noodles to a platter, and spread them out flat, overlapping as necessary. Make sure that all the noodles are lightly coated with oil, so they don't stick together. Refrigerate for 45 minutes before assembling the lasagna.

With a slotted spoon, remove all the meatballs and sausage from the sauce. Chop roughly or, preferably, pull apart into small chunks with your hands, and place in a bowl. Set a baking pan on a large work surface, with the sauce, chopped meat, ricotta mixture, noodles, Parmigiano, and Muenster cheese nearby.

Preheat the oven to 375°. Cover the bottom of the baking pan with ½ cup of the sauce, and top with a solid layer of noodles, laid lengthwise without overlapping. Sprinkle with ¼ cup Parmigiano. Drizzle 1 cup of the sauce over the pasta; then top with another layer of noodles and ¼ cup Parmigiano. Spoon on large dollops of the ricotta mixture, using about half (don't try to spread it evenly or the noodles will shift; the ricotta will spread out when cooked). Top with another layer of noodles and Parmigiano. Scatter half the chopped meat over the noodles, and cover evenly with 1 cup of sauce. Top with another layer of pasta and ¼ cup Parmigiano; then use half the Muenster to make an even layer all the way out to the edges.

Make another layer of noodles, top with ¼ cup Parmigiano, and spoon on the remaining ricotta. Scatter the remaining chopped meat, and drizzle evenly with 1 cup of sauce. Make a final layer of noodles, sauce, and Parmigiano, and a last, even layer of sliced Muenster. Refrigerate the remaining sauce until serving time.

Poke toothpicks into the lasagna every 3 inches around the edges of the pan to support a large piece of aluminum foil without letting it touch the surface of the cheese. Mold the edges of the foil down gently around the pan without tearing. Bake the lasagna for 30 minutes; then reduce the heat to 350° and cook for 40 minutes more. Remove from the oven, and remove (but don't discard) the foil. Let the lasagna stand uncovered at room temperature for 1 hour; then replace the foil and let stand for at least 3, and up to 4, hours at room temperature. This allows the lasagna to set, so that it firms up and slices easily. When properly set, a toothpick inserted in the center should meet some resistance; if it goes in easily, the cheese has not yet set.

Half an hour before serving, preheat the oven to 375°. Remove the foil, and bake the lasagna for 25 to 30 minutes, until quite warm at the center. Warm the remaining sauce, and serve on the side in a bowl. Slice the lasagna into squares, and serve on warmed plates. Don't forget to toast yourself for this major accomplishment. Everyone else will, too.

"This is 90 percent my mom's lasagna and 10 percent mine. Everyone in the family loved it. Most people would use oregano or basil, but my mother used bay leaves. That was her secret, and I was the only one who knew it. My sister still doesn't know. I changed the cheese to Muenster, but everything else is my mom's. I like the Muenster because it's much creamier and doesn't make the lasagna rubbery the way mozzarella does. If it has those orange edges, trim them away so you have clean white slices of cheese. As for the Parmigiano, you could substitute Pecorino-Romano if you like it better. Myself, I would never use a sheep's milk cheese.

"I call for 2 pounds of pasta. You may not need it all, but it's better to have too much than too little—otherwise you have to start the whole noodle-cooking process again. Be sure to shape the meatballs the day before so they can firm up. Otherwise the texture just doesn't work. Oh yeah, and when making meatballs, the meat and the bowl should be very cold, just as if you were making homemade sausage."

—Tony Tammero

— CHAPTER 7 —

Sides

When the first Palm opened in Manhattan, side dishes were minimal and very Italian: string beans marinara, plus anything that could be served Aglio e Olio. The restaurant's sides developed over time, based on what went well with steak. Some customers made requests, and others asked for a serving of "what those guys over there are having." Slowly, side dishes made it into the repertoire of offerings. Later, when a written menu debuted, the sides were defined and limited a little more. Because the kitchen has always had a policy of serving almost any dish a customer requests, side dishes (as with everything else) were selected on a truly democratic basis. Now they've all become bona fide classics, as much a part of the traditional steakhouse dinner as a juicy porterhouse itself.

CREAMED SPINACH

— SERVES 6 TO 8 —

Here, for the first time in print, is the definitive, time-tested, beloved recipe for all to enjoy. That said, it's worth noting that the chef at each Palm location likes to put his own spin on the legendary creamed spinach. The differences may be subtle, but they definitely exist.

2 (10-ounce) boxes frozen chopped spinach, completely thawed
2 tablespoons lightly salted butter
1½ cups heavy cream
1 teaspoon fine sea salt
½ teaspoon white pepper, preferably freshly ground

½ teaspoon ground nutmeg, preferably freshly ground
1 tablespoon cornstarch
1 tablespoon white wine, or water
1 cup grated Parmigiano-Reggiano

Using your hands, squeeze as much water as possible from the thawed spinach. In a large saucepan, combine the butter and cream over medium heat. When the butter has melted, stir in the spinach, salt, white pepper, and nutmeg. Stirring occasionally, bring the mixture to a simmer, and cook for 3 minutes. In a small bowl, blend the cornstarch and wine with your fingertips, so that you can feel when all the starch is dissolved. Add to the spinach mixture, and continue stirring until thickened, about 2 minutes. Stir in the Parmigiano, and taste for seasoning. Serve at once, or keep warm in the top of a covered double boiler over barely simmering water for up to 30 minutes.

"Everybody's worried about giving this recipe out. But I say, either you do it or you don't do it. If you use good butter, Parmigiano-Reggiano, and freshly ground nutmeg, you can make a great creamed spinach. I'm not saying it's going to be exactly like ours because there are, you know, variables at work in every kitchen."

—Tony Tammero, executive chef

LEAF SPINACH

— SERVES 4 —

Spinach is notorious for its ability to retain dirt in all its nooks and crannies, so Jeffrey Bleaken, chef at the Philadelphia Palm, insists on washing it at least twice. If you've ever bitten into a luscious mouthful of fresh spinach and encountered a piece of grit, you'll want to follow his advice.

"It's just wilted fresh leaves with a little chicken stock," says Tony Tammero of this recipe. "Simple, but everybody loves it."

2 pounds spinach, well washed and tough stems removed
Fine sea salt and freshly ground black pepper

¼ cup chicken stock
1 tablespoon unsalted butter, melted (optional)

With water clinging to its leaves, place the spinach in a large sauté pan. Cook, covered, over high heat, until the leaves on the bottom of the pan are wilted, about 3 minutes. Add ½ teaspoon salt and a few turns of the peppermill. Using tongs, turn the spinach and cover. Cook for 3 minutes more, until wilted. Transfer to a colander, and press down firmly to squeeze out some of the excess water. Wipe the pan with paper towels, add the spinach, and place over medium heat. Add the chicken stock, and cook, tossing frequently, for 1 minute. Serve at once, drizzled with a little melted butter, if desired.

Spinach Aglio e Olio

This dish has been in the Palm repertoire for generations. It's been tinkered with over the years: for instance, Tony used to chop the garlic, but some people complained that the flavor was too strong. This way, you can remove the cloves or leave them in, according to taste. Real garlic lovers will want to chop the cloves. The extra step of blanching the spinach is worth the effort, for the resulting silky texture and sweet, gentle flavor.

2 pounds spinach, well washed and tough stems removed

Kosher salt, for blanching the spinach

2 tablespoons olive oil

6 large garlic cloves, crushed with the side of a large, heavy knife

Fine sea salt

Bring a large saucepan full of lightly salted water to the boil. Add the spinach, and blanch for about 1 minute; then drain well in a colander and rinse with cold running water. When the spinach is cool enough to handle, use your hands to firmly squeeze out the excess water. In a large sauté pan, heat the olive oil over medium-high heat. Add the garlic, and sauté, stirring constantly, for about 3 minutes, until golden brown. Do not let the garlic burn. Add the spinach and ¼ teaspoon sea salt, and toss until heated through, about 2 minutes. Serve at once or, if desired, at room temperature.

"Based on my American Express card end-of-year summary, I am probably one of the biggest customers of the L.A. Palm. I go there because it's a great place to hang out. Nobody could make you feel warm and welcomed like Gigi could. The food is wonderful, of course, but after twenty years, it's not about the food. I grew up in Bensonhurst, in Brooklyn, and there's not a day or night when I've been to the [L.A.] Palm that I don't run into somebody I grew up with. Everybody is always there."

—*Sid Young, Los Angeles businessman and Palm aficionado*

String Beans Aglio e Olio

— Serves 4 to 6 —

Blanching in boiling water then shocking in ice water is the secret to brightly colored vegetables with vitamins intact. Far from making extra work, this technique actually gets the troublesome part of the cooking out of the way early, so all that's left to do at the last minute is toss the beans with the hot oil and garlic. As with many of the deceptively simple recipes in this book, top-quality ingredients and attention to timing will spell success. Note that kosher salt is used for cooking the pasta and vegetables, but for seasoning, the pricier and better-quality sea salt is called for.

Kosher salt, for blanching the beans
1 pound small green beans, ends trimmed
2 tablespoons olive oil

5 or 6 cloves garlic, crushed with the side of
 a large, heavy knife
Fine sea salt

Bring a large pot of water to a furious boil, and add 1 tablespoon of kosher salt. Have ready a large bowl filled with ice water.

Add the beans to the pot and cook, uncovered, for 4 to 6 minutes, depending on the thickness of the beans. Do not overcook; they should be almost tender but still retain a little snap. Drain the beans in a colander, and immediately plunge them into the ice water. Swirl until cooled; then drain thoroughly. If you don't plan to serve them immediately, spread the beans on a kitchen towel to dry; then cover with plastic wrap and refrigerate for up to 3 hours.

Place a large saucepan or sauté pan over medium heat, and add the oil. Add the garlic, and cook, stirring constantly, until the cloves just begin to turn golden. Do not let the garlic burn. Add the beans, and cook, tossing frequently, for about 2 minutes, until just warmed through. Remove and discard the larger pieces of garlic (or use for salad dressing, if desired). Season the beans with a pinch of sea salt, and serve at once.

"There are two vegetables that you cook soft: string beans and broccoli raab, because it gives more flavor. (I mean the bigger string beans, not those little haricots verts.) If you make the strings beans al dente—crispy—it sucks. No flavor. Cooking them more brings out the natural sugars and sweetness. People don't know that—they think all vegetables, especially the green ones, have to be al dente. If they only knew! First I boil the string beans until they're a little soft, but definitely not mushy. Then when I'm ready to serve, I make a little aglio olio in a pan, with some black pepper—that's the best. Maybe a little butter, or just extra-virgin olive oil. Then you add the beans and cook them very slowly, no browning, just enough for the sweetness. I love broccoli raab, but when I get it in restaurants, it's always hard —I have to send it back. We do a broccoli raab Parmesan sometimes. After it's soft, you stick it in the broiler with the cheese and it comes out all crispy."

STRING BEANS MARINARA

— SERVES 4 TO 6 —

If beans bore you, this simple dish will be a revelation. Marinara is one of those "frying-pan sauces" that just takes a few minutes to prepare. The beans become sweet, tender, and lightly caramelized in the simple but flavorful sauce. This is a truly great accompaniment for a simple, perfect steak.

Kosher salt, for blanching the beans
1 pound green beans, ends trimmed
2 tablespoons olive oil

¾ cup Marinara Sauce (page 146), or best-quality bottled marinara

Bring a large pot of water to a furious boil, and add 1 tablespoon of salt. Have ready a large bowl filled with ice water.

Add the beans, and cook, uncovered, for 4 to 6 minutes, depending on the thickness of the beans. Do not overcook; they should be almost tender but still retain a little snap. Drain the beans in a colander, and immediately plunge them into the ice water. Swirl until cooled; then drain thoroughly. If you don't plan to serve them immediately, spread the beans on a kitchen towel to dry; then cover with plastic wrap and refrigerate for up to 3 hours.

Place a large saucepan or sauté pan over medium heat, and add the oil. Add the beans, and cook for about 4 minutes, tossing occasionally, until just beginning to color. Add the Marinara Sauce, and cook, tossing occasionally, until the beans are tender and the sauce clings to them, about 2 minutes more. Serve at once, or cover and keep in a warm place, but away from direct heat, for up to 10 minutes.

BROCCOLI RAAB PARMIGIANO-REGGIANO

— SERVES 4 —

One of the quintessential Italian vegetables, broccoli raab is now widely available, and not only to restaurants. "We used to serve broccoli raab just simple, aglio olio, but I know how Americans get excited when they start thinking about melted cheese, so I turned it into Parmigiano." —Tony Tammero, executive chef

Kosher salt, for blanching the broccoli raab
1¼ pounds broccoli raab, tough lower stems
*   trimmed*
2 tablespoons olive oil
6 large cloves garlic, crushed with the side of
*   a large, heavy knife*

Fine sea salt
½ teaspoon crushed red pepper flakes
1 cup grated Parmigiano-Reggiano

Bring a large saucepan of salted water to the boil. Add the broccoli raab, and blanch for about 4 minutes, until barely tender. Drain and place on a baking sheet lined with paper towels. If desired, cover with plastic wrap and refrigerate for up to 3 hours.

Preheat the oven to 450°. If the broccoli raab has been refrigerated, bring it to room temperature for 10 minutes.

In a large saute pan, heat the olive oil over medium-high heat. Add the garlic, and sauté, stirring constantly, for about 3 minutes, until golden. Do not let the garlic burn. Add ½ teaspoon salt and the red pepper, and stir for 1 minute more. Add the blanched broccoli raab, reduce the heat to medium-low, and cook, turning occasionally, for about 3 minutes. Do not brown. Lightly oil a shallow baking dish large enough to hold the broccoli raab in one layer. Transfer the broccoli raab to the baking dish, scatter evenly with the Parmigiano, and bake for 6 to 8 minutes, until the cheese is crisped and golden.

HASH BROWNS

— SERVES 4 —

If possible, steam the potatoes one day (or even two) before you plan to serve these hash browns. If that isn't feasible, make sure the steamed potatoes are thoroughly cooled to room temperature; then refrigerate for at least 1 hour before proceeding with the recipe.

1½ *pounds red potatoes, about 6*
¼ *cup Clarified Butter (page 32)*

Fine sea salt and freshly ground black pepper
1 *tablespoon finely chopped flat-leaf parsley*

Steam the potatoes over simmering water for about 20 minutes, until firm but yielding to the point of a sharp knife. Cool to room temperature. Cut the unpeeled potatoes into ⅜-inch strips; then cut crosswise into cubes about ½ inch square.

Place a large nonstick skillet over medium heat, and add 2 tablespoons of the clarified butter. When the butter is hot, add the potatoes and spread them quickly into an even layer. Season with ¼ teaspoon salt and two turns of the peppermill. Use a wide, flat spatula to press the potatoes down firmly. Cook, pressing down occasionally, for 6 to 7 minutes, or until the bottom is golden brown and crisp. Reduce the heat slightly if the potatoes begin to burn.

Place a large plate over the top of the skillet, and hold it securely with one hand. Using an oven mitt on the other hand, and with a firm grip on the skillet handle, quickly invert the hash browns onto the plate. Add the remaining 2 tablespoons of clarified butter to the pan, and slide the hash browns back into the pan with the cooked side up. Season with ¼ teaspoon salt. Cook, pressing down occasionally, until golden brown and crisp, 5 to 6 minutes more. Transfer the hash browns to a cutting board or platter, and blot the surface gently with paper towels. Cut in quarters and serve at once, sprinkling a little parsley in the center of each serving.

Mashed Potatoes

"I don't know if we're famous for this," says Tony Tammero, "but we sure sell a ton of it."

2½ pounds Idaho or russet potatoes, peeled
   and quartered
Kosher salt, for cooking the potatoes
3 ounces lightly salted butter, cut into
   6 chunks, at room temperature

½ cup half-and-half, warmed
Fine sea salt and white pepper, preferably
   freshly ground

In a large saucepan, cover the potatoes with lightly salted water. Bring to a boil over high heat; then reduce to a simmer, and cook until fork-tender, about 20 minutes. Drain thoroughly, shaking to eliminate excess water. Return to the pan, and immediately add the butter, the warm half-and-half, and ½ teaspoon sea salt. Using a potato masher or a hand-held blender, mash the potatoes until they are just slightly lumpy. Add pepper to taste, stir well, and taste for seasoning. Add more salt, if desired. Serve at once, or cover and keep warm in the top of a double boiler over simmering water for up to 30 minutes.

"I love mashed potatoes, but Louie [Luigi "Gigi" Delmaestro] didn't want Martine, the chef at the West Hollywood Palm, to make them because it took too much time. 'It's not on the menu, period,' he would say to me. So one time I'm pleading with the waiter to have Martine make me mashed potatoes without telling Louie, and a little while later Louie comes out of the kitchen with a platter of mashed potatoes, big smile on his face. 'Who ordered the mashed potatoes at this table?' I raised my hand, and I got them. I got them right in the face. And I ate them all."

—Bob Bro, Los Angeles businessman

HALF AND HALF

This is one of those dishes that made it onto the menu through the power of the people—the customers who adore both the Palm's Fried Onions and Cottage Fries, especially when combined. Admittedly, this is easier to make in a restaurant kitchen, with great big fryers that are always filled with oil at the right temperature. But if you have a deep fryer at home and love to fry, dig in!

Is the double-cooking technique important? Absolutely. The first phase cooks the potatoes all the way though to the center; then the second phase crisps and browns the outside. If you tried to cook them through all at once, the outside would burn before the inside became tender. If you cooked the potatoes for a longer time at the lower temperature, they would absorb way too much oil.

Canola oil, for deep frying (about 3 quarts)
1½ pounds large onions, prepared and fried once as per the recipe for Fried Onions (page 173)

1½ pounds russet potatoes, prepared and fried once as per the recipe for Cottage Fries (page 170)
Fine sea salt

Place enough oil in a deep fryer or a wide 10- to 12-quart stockpot to come halfway up the sides of the pot, and heat it to 375° on a candy/deep-fat thermometer. Using a skimmer or a fryer basket, slowly lower the Fried Onions into the oil. Fry, nudging occasionally with a skimmer to help them brown evenly, until the onions are crisp and golden brown, about 5 minutes. (The temperature of the oil will drop when you first add the potatoes; keep the heat high and, if necessary, regulate it to remain near 375°, but no hotter.) Scoop up the onions with the skimmer, shaking the excess oil back into the pot, and transfer to a large, rimmed baking sheet lined with paper towels. Keep warm in a low oven. When the oil returns to 375°, lower the Cottage Fries into the oil, and fry until crisp and golden, about 2 minutes. Scoop up the potatoes with the skimmer, shaking the excess oil back into the pot, and drain on fresh paper towels, as above. Toss with the Fried Onions and a little salt, and serve at once, preferably on heated plates.

Baked Potatoes

— Serves 4 —

Baking the potatoes directly on an oven rack, instead of in a pan, allows the formation of a lovely, crisp skin all the way around. This is the simplest of dishes, but one in which the proper ingredients and techniques are crucial to success.

4 very large (12 to 14 ounces each) Idaho or
    russet potatoes, scrubbed and dried with
    paper towels
¼ cup unsalted butter, softened

Coarse sea salt
½ to 1 cup sour cream
¼ cup finely snipped chives

Preheat the oven to 425°.

Rub the potatoes all over with softened butter. Sprinkle with coarse salt, and place the potatoes directly on the top oven rack. Place a rimmed baking sheet on the rack below, and pour in about ¼ cup water (so that when the butter drips and hits the pan, it doesn't smoke). Bake the potatoes for 1 hour and 15 minutes, until tender when pierced with a small knife or toothpick. Divide the sour cream between 4 ramekins. Sprinkle the sour cream with chives, and serve 1 ramekin on the side of each potato.

"**Never cook baked potatoes in foil. On a rack, you don't get that soggy spot—the potato is crisp all over.**"

—Tony Tammero, executive chef

Potatoes Lyonnaise

— Serves 6 —

This is a wildly popular dish, but old Palm hands may have noticed that it changes from restaurant to restaurant. The exact formula is left up to the chef, and each has his favorite. This version is the most traditional, as prepared by Brian McCardle at Palms One and Too in Manhattan.

Kosher salt, for cooking the potatoes
1½ pounds red bliss or other red potatoes, scrubbed
1 cup peanut oil
¼ cup Clarified Butter (page 32)

2 medium onions, root ends trimmed, halved lengthwise, and thinly sliced lengthwise
Fine sea salt and freshly ground black pepper
1 tablespoon finely chopped flat-leaf parsley, for garnish

Bring a large pot of salted water to a boil. Add the potatoes, and boil until they are tender when pierced with the tip of a knife but not falling apart, about 10 minutes. Drain the potatoes; when they are cool enough to handle, slice ¼ inch thick.

Place a large sauté pan over high heat, and add the oil. Add the sliced potatoes and cook, turning once, until golden brown on both sides. Don't turn too often, or they will start to break up. Remove the browned potatoes with a slotted spoon, and set aside.

Discard the peanut oil, and return the pan to medium heat. Add the clarified butter; when it is hot, add the onions. Cook, stirring occasionally, for about 12 minutes, until golden brown. Add the reserved potatoes, ½ teaspoon salt, and a few turns of the peppermill. Cook for 3 or 4 minutes, turning occasionally, until the potatoes are crusted on the outside but still retain their shape. Garnish with parsley, and serve at once.

"Wherever I travel, I check to see if there is a Palm. I've been to them all—the food is just great! Of course, New York is my favorite, because I can get my 'Palm fix' right here at home."

—Mrs. Abraham (Casey) Ribicoff, New York City

COTTAGE FRIES

— SERVES 4 TO 6 —

There is nothing like the flavor of these perfect, crisp, golden fries. To achieve optimum crispness, they're fried twice, the first time to cook them through to the center, and the second time to crisp them up. Deep frying at home can be a messy, potentially dangerous business. Be sure that the oil comes only halfway up the sides of the pan, because it will bubble up alarmingly (and possibly over, in a smaller pan) when the potatoes are first added (see Note). Keep children away from the stove area when deep frying, and have copious amount of paper towels on hand. Then, dig in and enjoy!

1½ pounds Idaho or russet potatoes, peeled
Vegetable or canola oil, for deep frying
   (about 3 quarts)

Fine sea salt

Using a mandoline or a very sharp knife, slice the potatoes lengthwise about ⅛ inch thick. Place the slices in a large bowl in the kitchen sink, and let lukewarm water run slowly into the bowl, rinsing the potatoes until the water spilling over the edges runs clear (about 20 minutes). Make sure all the potatoes are submerged. Let the potatoes stand in the clear water at room temperature for about 2 hours, to remove as much starch as possible. (If desired, they may be refrigerated in the bowl of water overnight.) Rinse the potatoes under fast-running, very hot tap water to remove the remaining starch. Shake dry in a colander, and spread on a large kitchen towel. Pat dry gently but thoroughly.

Place enough oil in a deep fryer or a wide 10- to 12-quart stockpot to come halfway up the sides of the pot, and heat it to 375° on a candy/deep-fat thermometer. Using a skimmer or a fryer basket, slowly lower the potatoes into the oil (the oil will bubble up quite a bit at first). Fry, nudging with a skimmer occasionally to help them brown evenly, until the potatoes are pale golden brown, about 7 minutes. (The temperature of the oil will drop when you first add the potatoes; keep the heat high and, if necessary, regulate it to remain near 375°, but no hotter.) Scoop up the potatoes with the skimmer, shaking the excess oil back into the pot, and transfer to a large, rimmed baking sheet lined with 2 layers of paper towels. Let cool for at least 30 minutes before frying again. The potatoes may also be stored in an airtight container at room temperature for up to 8 hours before the second frying.

When ready to serve, reheat the oil to 375°. Add the potatoes, and fry until crisp and golden but not dark brown, 2 to 3 minutes. Remove with the skimmer, and drain briefly on fresh paper towels. Sprinkle with several pinches of salt, and serve at once, preferably on heated plates.

Note: If, despite your best precautions, a large quantity of oil bubbles over the edge of the pan, turn off a gas burner immediately. If using an electric stove, quickly but very carefully use potholders to remove the pan from the hot element. Oil can catch fire quickly when exposed to a direct heat source. Use a large quantity of flour or old towels—never water—to smother an oil fire.

SWEET POTATO COTTAGE FRIES

— SERVES 4 —

This is one of those dishes that are nearly impossible to make without a mandoline. There are several models available now, including a few that will not require you to mortgage your house or take a second job. That said, however, the big, expensive, professional mandolines are definitely the way to go if you like crisp, thinly sliced vegetables. In that case, you may as well buy a home deep frying appliance, too. The frying process is much easier with a large quantity of temperature-controlled oil. In a smaller pan, the potatoes run the risk of sticking together, but you can discourage this by nudging them with extra-long-handled tongs or your skimmer basket. If you opt to use a standard cooking pot for deep frying, exercise extreme caution around the hot oil and keep the kitchen free of onlookers and helpers, particularly young, mobile children (see Note).

3 sweet potatoes, about 1¾ pounds, scrubbed, with skins left on

Peanut oil for deep frying (about 1 gallon)
Fine sea salt

Slice the potatoes very thinly, about a scant ⅛ inch. Place the slices in a large bowl, and cover them with hot tap water. Make sure all the slices are submerged. Let the potatoes stand for 1½ hours to remove some of the starch, which might otherwise burn. Rinse the potatoes under fast-running, very hot tap water to remove the remaining starch. Shake dry in a colander, and spread flat on a double layer of paper towels. Place another double layer of paper towels on top, and press all the potatoes firmly to blot up as much moisture as possible. (A wet potato will "spit" when added to hot oil!)

Place enough oil in a deep fryer or a wide 10- to 12-quart stockpot to come halfway up the sides of the pot, and heat it to 325° on a candy/deep-fat thermometer. Using a skimmer or a fryer basket, slowly lower the potatoes into the oil (the oil will bubble up quite a bit at first). Fry, nudging with a skimmer occasionally to help them brown evenly, until they are golden brown, 12 to 14 minutes. (The temperature of the oil will drop when you first add the potatoes; keep the heat high and, if necessary, regulate it to remain near 325°, but no hotter.) Scoop up the sweet potatoes with the skimmer, shaking the excess oil back into the pot, and transfer to a large, rimmed baking sheet lined with 2 layers of paper towels. Let cool for at least 30 minutes before frying again. The potatoes may also be stored in an airtight container at room temperature for up to 8 hours before the second frying.

When ready to serve, reheat the oil to 350°. Add the potatoes, and fry for about 1 minute, but no more—just long enough to crisp and warm them through. Remove with the skimmer, and drain briefly on fresh paper towels. Sprinkle with several pinches of salt, and serve at once, preferably on heated plates.

Note: If, despite your best precautions, a large quantity of oil bubbles over the edge of the pan, turn off a gas burner immediately. If using an electric stove, quickly but very carefully use potholders to remove the pan from the hot element. Oil can catch fire quickly when exposed to a direct heat source. Use a large quantity of flour or old towels—never water—to smother an oil fire.

FRENCH-FRIED ONIONS

— SERVES 4 —

These delicious, crisp (and fattening) onions go great with just about anything: roasted chicken, fish, and, of course, a nice juicy steak Palm-style. Be sure to fill the pan only half full with oil—it will bubble up alarmingly (and in a smaller pot, possibly over) when the potatoes are first added (see Note). Keep children away from the stove area when deep frying, and have copious amount of paper towels on hand.

2 pounds yellow onions, peeled
Peanut oil for deep frying (about 3 quarts)

2 cups all-purpose flour
Fine sea salt

Using a mandoline or a sharp knife, slice the onions very thinly. The slices should be less than ⅛ inch thick, but not so thin that the rings are incomplete.

Place enough oil in a deep fryer or a wide 10- to 12-quart stockpot to come halfway up the sides of the pot, and heat it to 375° on a candy/deep-fat thermometer.

In a large bowl, combine the onions with the flour, and toss, separating them into circular sections and coating all the rings evenly. Transfer the onion rings to a colander, and shake gently to remove any excess or clumped flour. Using a skimmer or a fryer basket, lower the onions into the hot oil, and stir constantly with a skimmer until pale golden brown, 3 to 4 minutes. Remove with the skimmer, shaking the excess oil back into the pot, and drain on a double layer of paper towels for at least 30 minutes. The onions may also be stored in an airtight container at room temperature for up to 8 hours before the second frying.

When ready to serve, reheat the oil to 375°. Add the onion rings and fry until crisp and golden brown, 30 seconds to 1 minute, stirring constantly. Remove with the skimmer and drain briefly on fresh paper towels. Sprinkle with several pinches of salt, and serve at once, preferably on heated plates.

SAUTÉED MUSHROOMS

— SERVES 4 —

Mushrooms shrink quite a bit during cooking because they contain so much water. The cooking process also concentrates the flavor, producing these very simple but luscious, mushroomy nuggets that complement a good steak.

12 large, firm white mushrooms, brushed
    clean, stem ends trimmed flush
¼ cup Clarified Butter (page 32)
2 tablespoons fresh lemon juice
¼ cup dry white wine

¼ cup chicken stock
Fine sea salt
2 tablespoons unsalted butter, at room
    temperature

Preheat the broiler to high heat. Place the mushrooms, rounded sides up, in a large, ovenproof sauté pan that will fit under your broiler. Brush the tops liberally with the clarified butter, and place under the hot broiler until golden brown. Transfer the pan to the stovetop over high heat, and add the lemon juice and white wine. Simmer for 6 minutes, until the liquid has reduced by half; then add the chicken stock. Continue simmering until the liquid has again reduced by half, about 4 minutes. Season with a little salt, and swirl in the butter, shaking the pan vigorously to emulsify the sauce. Using tongs, transfer the mushrooms to individual plates or a serving platter, and drizzle with the sauce.

Everybody, without exception, is thrilled to get their caricature drawn on the wall at the Palm, though a common complaint is, "My portrait makes me look fat." One female celebrity was escorted out of the Philadelphia Palm when she was caught adding eye makeup to her portrait. Someone once drew a steak knife in the hand of O.J. Simpson on the wall at the Dallas Palm. The knife was removed, but the picture remains, as it does in the L.A. Palm, though no one likes to talk about it. There is no way to influence the choice of who gets their face on the wall; it has to do with frequency of attendance, and how much the staff likes you. Celebrity alone is not a motivating factor. Although Tony Tammero says, "The only way to guarantee getting your face on the wall is to marry Wally."

— CHAPTER 8 —

Dishes Made with Leftovers

Let's face it—even a perfect steak or lobster can sometimes be too much to eat all at once. Consequently, the Palm does a brisk business in doggie bags, elegantly printed with the restaurant's name and logo. In fact, they go through 500,000 take-home bags each year. The recipes in this chapter were designed to take delicious advantage of those leftovers. Instead of just nibbling at a cold steak (or worse, forgetting about it after it gets pushed to the back of the refrigerator shelf), try making a creative salad to serve one or two people. Or make a classic roast beef hash, a pot of chili, or a shepherd's pie. Unlike those in other chapters, most of these recipes do not come from the kitchens of the Palm, but from that of the author, who brought home many Palm doggie bags in the course of researching this book. If you're simply cooking up a great steak from scratch, any of the salads in this chapter would make a superb and refreshing accompaniment.

STEAK SALAD WITH "AU JUS" DRESSING, TOMATOES, AND ROMAINE

— SERVES 1 —

No matter how fabulous the meat might have been, perhaps it was just a little too much to finish the night before. With this simple, straightforward salad that highlights a great piece of steak, you get to enjoy it twice.

Place the consomme on the heat to reduce, and remove the steak from the refrigerator about 35 minutes before you plan to dine. This recipe can easily be doubled, in the event that your doggie bag is particularly well endowed.

1 10½-ounce can beef consomme
4 to 5 ounces cooked New York strip, porterhouse, or filet steak, at room temperature

Pale, inner heart of 1 romaine lettuce head, torn into large, bite-sized pieces
1 ripe beefsteak tomato, cored and cut into ¾-inch cubes (including juice and seeds)

1 tablespoon canola oil

¼ teaspoon fine sea salt

Freshly ground black pepper

1 to 2 teaspoons white wine vinegar

In a small saucepan, bring the consomme to a simmer over medium-high heat. Simmer briskly until reduced by half, 10 to 15 minutes. Remove from the heat, and pour into a Pyrex measuring cup to help the liquid cool faster. When the reduced consomme has reached room temperature, after about 20 minutes, proceed with the recipe.

Slice the cooked steak across the grain, on the diagonal, ¼ inch thick. In a large bowl, combine the romaine, tomato, oil, salt, black pepper to taste, and 4 tablespoons of the reduced consomme (save the remaining consomme reduction for your next soup or sauce). Toss thoroughly, and drizzle with 1 teaspoon of the vinegar. Toss again and taste a leaf, adding the second teaspoon of vinegar, if necessary, and tossing again. Using tongs, mound the salad on a large plate, and drape the sliced steak on top. Season with black pepper, and serve at once.

CALIFORNIA STEAK SALAD WITH RED ONIONS, WATERCRESS, TANGERINES, AND BLACK PEPPER VINAIGRETTE

— SERVES 2 —

This salad can be prepared quite successfully without leftover meat, in which case it makes a crisp and refreshing accompaniment to a just-seared steak.

½ medium red onion, root end trimmed, thinly sliced lengthwise

1½ tablespoons white wine vinegar

2 teaspoons Dijon mustard

1 teaspoon coarsely cracked black pepper

¼ teaspoon fine sea salt

¼ cup extra-virgin olive oil

6 to 8 ounces cooked New York strip, porterhouse, or filet steak, at room temperature

2 tangerines, peel and pith removed with a sharp knife, cut into segments between the membranes

2 bunches watercress, coarse stems removed, washed, and dried

Freshly ground black pepper

In a bowl, cover the sliced onion with ice water, and soak for 30 to 45 minutes to crisp and mellow the flavor. Meanwhile, make the vinaigrette: In a glass bowl, combine the vinegar, mustard, cracked pepper, and ¼ teaspoon salt, and whisk until thoroughly blended. Drizzle in the olive oil in a thin stream, whisking constantly until all the oil has been added and the mixture is emulsified. Slice the steak across the grain, on the diagonal, ¼ inch thick.

Drain the red onions well, and pat them dry with paper towels. In a large bowl, gently toss the tangerine segments with the watercress. Drizzle with just enough vinaigrette to coat, and toss again. Using tongs, divide the salad between two plates, and scatter a few onion rings on top. Drape the sliced steak around the edges of each salad, season with a few turns of the peppermill, and serve at once.

"My husband, Brian, and I have been coming to the Los Angeles Palm since it opened back in 1975, and we've always felt that it was our home away from home. Gigi was like family, and so are Wally and Bruce. Brian and I even got married at Wally's ranch in Colorado. When the West Side Palm opened in New York, we fell in love with the ambiance and the staff there as well. We've known Bruce Jr. since he was a young teenager, and now seeing his generation take over gives me a lot of hope that the Palm will remain a sensational place."

—Cheryl Ladd

STEAK SALAD WITH BUTTER LETTUCE, GRUYERE CROÛTES, AND NIÇOISE OLIVES

— SERVES 2 —

Lacking leftovers, this salad is also lovely with a freshly grilled or sautéed steak. You will really go for it if you like a little French influence with your Prime beef.

2 thin slices sourdough bread

Olive oil, for brushing the bread

Fine sea salt and freshly ground black pepper

1 tablespoon grated Gruyere cheese

6 to 8 ounces cooked New York strip,
porterhouse, or filet steak, at room
temperature

1 tablespoon red wine vinegar or fresh
lemon juice

2 teaspoons Dijon mustard

2½ tablespoons extra-virgin olive oil

Inner leaves of 1 head butter lettuce, washed,
dried, and torn into bite-sized pieces

6 Niçoise olives, pitted and quartered
lengthwise

Preheat the oven to 350°. Place the bread slices on a baking sheet, and brush with the olive oil. Season with salt and pepper, and scatter evenly with the Gruyere. Bake for about 10 minutes, until the cheese is melted.

Slice the steak across the grain, on the diagonal, ¼ inch thick. In a large bowl, combine the vinegar, mustard, ¼ teaspoon salt, a generous grinding of pepper, and the extra-virgin olive oil. Whisk until the dressing is emulsified; then add the lettuce, and toss thoroughly until all the leaves are evenly coated, but not drenched, with the dressing.

Using tongs, divide the salad between two plates, and scatter each one with half of the quartered olives. Fan the sliced steak on one edge of the salad, and place a Gruyere croûte on the other side. Serve at once.

Thai Steak Salad with Basil and Mint

— Serves 2 —

And now, the Thai version of "fabulous things to do with leftover steak." If you decide to make this dish from scratch, without a doggie bag of cold steak on hand, you should still marinate the cooked meat in the zipper-lock bag. The resulting flavor will be incredible, like a Thai version of the delicious Japanese dish beef tataki.

MARINADE:

1 tablespoon soy sauce

1 tablespoon Thai fish sauce (see Note)

1 tablespoon rice vinegar

1 stalk lemongrass, pale inner heart only,
sliced paper-thin

SALAD:

6 to 8 ounces cooked New York strip,
  porterhouse, or filet steak

4 ounces (about 4 cups) baby field greens
  (use an Asian mix, if available), washed
  and dried

Unblemished leaves from 1 small bunch
  fresh basil, about ¾ cup, loosely packed

¼ cup fresh mint leaves

3 tablespoons canola oil

Fine sea salt and freshly ground pepper

2 tablespoons rice vinegar

4 to 6 shiitake mushrooms, brushed clean
  and sliced

Deep-fried Wonton Skins, for garnish
  (optional, recipe below)

In a large zipper-lock bag, combine the soy sauce, fish sauce, 1 tablespoon rice vinegar, and lemongrass. Add the cooked steak, and seal the bag tightly. Refrigerate for at least 4 hours, or overnight. One hour before you plan to serve the salad, remove the bag from the refrigerator and allow the steak to come to room temperature.

Chill two large plates in the refrigerator. Remove the steak from the bag, and discard the marinade. Slice the steak across the grain, on the diagonal, ¼ inch thick.

In a large bowl, combine the baby greens with the basil and mint leaves. Drizzle with the canola oil and toss thoroughly to coat each leaf evenly. Season with ¼ teaspoon salt and a few turns of the peppermill, and drizzle with the rice vinegar. Add the sliced mushrooms, toss again thoroughly, and taste for seasoning.

Using tongs, divide the salad between the chilled plates, and drape the sliced steak on top. Serve at once, garnished with the Deep-Fried Wonton Skins, if desired.

Note: Thai fish sauce is available in Asian grocery stores and well-stocked supermarkets.

Deep-Fried Wonton Skins

Canola or other flavorless oil, for frying

5 wonton skins (wrappers), sliced into
  ½-inch strips

Heat about 2 inches of oil in a large skillet until hot but not smoking. Toss the wonton strips between your fingers to separate them, and carefully add them to the pan. Toss with tongs until crisp and golden, about 1 minute. Drain briefly on paper towels; then use at once, or let cool and store in an airtight container overnight, at room temperature, before using.

"When the Palm started, 'Prime' wasn't something you talked about—it wasn't a selling point. We were *serving* Prime, but even ten years ago it wasn't on the menu. Hey, there *was* no menu. It was just a given: we always bought the best-quality steak we could get. Now, there are a lot of steakhouses out there, and some of them *do* things to their steaks to provide a consistent flavor. Even Grade A Prime steaks can fluctuate from day to day. We noticed that some of the better steakhouses were using seasoning, and we weren't.

"So we came up with a garlic thing, and we went through phases where we tried various other seasoning concepts. What we realized was that nothing tastes better than a great steak with nothing on it. If you have an OK steak, then maybe a little seasoning is the way to go. So we just went back to the basic formula: make sure you have a great steak. That's why we have our own meat supplier. Just a little salt and a bit of drawn butter to give it a little sheen. And you unwrap the steaks the night before to let the surface dry a little. A wet steak doesn't sear right."

—Fred Thimm, *Palm president and COO*

Cold Sliced Steak with Salsa Verde

— Serves 1 or 2 —

There are many interpretations of salsa verde in the world—Mexico alone has quite a few, in fact—but this is one of my favorite Italian versions. Add a minced anchovy if you like. This sauce is just as fabulous with freshly cooked steak.

2 cloves garlic, thinly sliced
1 large bunch flat-leaf parsley, stemmed
   (about 3 cups loosely packed leaves)
½ cup loosely packed basil or mint leaves
2 tablespoons capers, drained
1 tablespoon Dijon mustard

1 tablespoon red wine vinegar
⅔ cup extra-virgin olive oil
4 to 6 ounces cooked New York strip,
   porterhouse, or filet steak, at room
   temperature

In a small food processor, combine the garlic, parsley, basil or mint, capers, mustard, and vinegar. Process to a paste, scraping down the sides. With the machine running, drizzle in half of the olive oil in a slow, steady steam. Stop the processor, and scrape down the sides of the bowl; then continue drizzling in the oil with the machine running until all the oil has been absorbed. (This sauce may be refrigerated in a covered container for up to 3 days before using, but the bright green color will fade after the first day.)

Slice the steak across the grain, on the diagonal, ¼ inch thick. Fan the slices across 1 or 2 plates. Spoon some of the salsa verde on top, and serve with a small green salad or buttered noodles, or both.

Open-Faced Filet Mignon Sandwich with Roasted Peppers, Fried Eggplant, and Fontina

— Serves 4 —

This is one way to extend a little leftover steak to feed four people. Of course, you can substitute fire-roasted peppers in a jar, if you prefer. For that matter, you can also pick up some grilled eggplant from your local gourmet market, and the sandwich practically makes itself!

Roasted Peppers:
4 red bell peppers, halved, cored, and seeded
2 large cloves garlic, crushed with the side
 of a large, heavy knife

2 tablespoons olive oil

Fried Eggplant:
1 large globe eggplant
1 tablespoon fine sea salt

⅓ cup olive oil

Sandwich:
6 to 8 ounces cooked filet steak, at room
 temperature
4 large, oval slices Italian bread

2 tablespoons mayonnaise (optional)
Freshly ground black pepper
½ pound sliced fontina cheese

Preheat the oven to 250°. In a roasting pan, toss the peppers with the garlic and olive oil. Season with salt and pepper; then roast for about 2 hours, until completely tender. Remove from the oven, cover the pan tightly with foil, and let stand for 20 minutes. Peel the peppers (try to remove all the skin, but don't worry if a little remains). Cut into quarters lengthwise, and set aside. Discard the garlic.

Slice the eggplant about ⅜ inch thick. Salt both sides of each slice liberally, and drain in a colander for 20 minutes. Press down firmly to extract the excess liquid, and wipe off the salt with paper towels. Place a large, heavy sauté pan over medium-low heat, and add the olive oil. Fry the eggplant, in batches if necessary to avoid overcrowding, until golden and softened, 5 to 6 minutes on each side. Remove with tongs, and drain on paper towels.

Slice the steak thinly, across the grain, ¼ inch thick. Place the bread on a baking sheet lined with foil, and preheat the broiler. Spread one side of each bread slice thinly with mayonnaise, if desired. Top with some of the sliced steak, a slice of eggplant, and a few pieces of red pepper. Season generously with black pepper, and top with a few slices of fontina. Broil just until the cheese melts, and serve at once.

ROAST BEEF HASH

— SERVES 3 TO 4 —

This tasty hash has successfully been made with the narrow tail-trimmings of filet mignon, which are always in abundance in a good steakhouse kitchen and sometimes available at a butcher shop. If preparing from scratch, cut the meat into ½-inch dice and sauté in a little canola oil over high heat until golden brown on the outside and pink inside, about 4 minutes total, turning once or twice. Cool slightly, and proceed with the recipe.

3 tablespoons olive oil
4 large red potatoes (1¼ pounds), washed,
   unpeeled, and cut into ½-inch dice
½ red onion, finely chopped
½ red bell pepper, cored, seeded, and cut
   into ½-inch dice

2 cloves garlic, crushed with the side of
   a large, heavy knife and finely chopped
Fine sea salt and freshly ground black pepper
1 pound cooked roast beef or prime rib,
   cut into ½-inch dice (about 2½ cups)
Poached eggs, for serving (optional)

Place a large, well-seasoned cast iron or nonstick skillet over medium-high heat, and add the olive oil. When the oil is hot but not smoking, add the potatoes, and sauté, turning frequently with a spatula, until they are crisp and golden all over, about 10 minutes.

Add the onion and pepper, and cook, turning, for 5 minutes more, until the vegetables are golden. Add the garlic, 1 teaspoon salt, and a generous grinding of black pepper, and cook for 1 minute more. Add the cooked, diced beef, increase the heat to high, and turn the mixture to combine. Spread in an even layer, and press down firmly with the spatula. After about 5 minutes, the bottom of the hash should be slightly charred, with a golden crust. Carefully turn the hash, in as few pieces as possible, and cook for a few minutes more without stirring. Serve immediately, topped with a poached egg, if desired.

UPTOWN CHILE CON CARNE

— SERVES 3 TO 4 —

The sauce in this chile is smooth, glossy, and deep, dark red. It is a very satisfying destination for a lonely leftover steak. Tony Tammero says, "Yeah, that's the way I make chile, but I'd never have any leftover steak, so I'd make it with beef chuck."

2 tablespoons canola or other vegetable oil
1 large onion, coarsely chopped
4 cloves garlic, crushed with the side of
   a large, heavy knife and finely chopped
2 tablespoons best-quality chile powder
1 teaspoon ground cumin
½ teaspoon dried oregano
½ teaspoon red pepper flakes

½ cup tomato paste
3 cups beef stock or consomme, homemade
   or canned
Fine sea salt and freshly ground black pepper
2 pounds cooked roast beef, prime rib, or
   New York strip steak, cut into ½-inch dice
Cooked beans and warm tortillas or rice,
   for serving

Place a Dutch oven or wide, heavy pot over medium heat, and add the oil. Add the onion and garlic, and sauté, stirring occasionally, for about 5 minutes, until softened. Remove from the heat, and add the chile powder, cumin, oregano, red pepper flakes, and tomato paste. Stir to form a paste; then add the beef stock, ¾ teaspoon salt, and a generous grinding of black pepper. Stir to combine, add the diced beef, and return to the heat.

Bring the mixture to a boil, stirring once or twice. Reduce the heat to a simmer, and partially cover the pot. Simmer for 1 hour, until the meat is tender and the sauce is thickened. Serve with warm beans on the side, accompanied by warm tortillas or, if you prefer, rice.

STEAK AND BRAISED ONIONS UNDER A PARMESAN CRUST

My sophisticated recipe-tasting family considers this the high point in the leftover firmament. Although there are a lot of ingredients, the recipe couldn't be easier. All the supporting players add up to a real blockbuster: meaty flavor, sweet onions, and a cheesy crust.

1 tablespoon salted butter

1 tablespoon olive oil

1 large onion, coarsely chopped

3 canned, peeled Italian plum tomatoes, squeezed to remove seeds, and coarsely chopped

2 teaspoons all-purpose flour

1 cup beef stock or consomme, homemade or canned

8 ounces cooked prime rib, roast beef, or steak, cut into ½-inch dice

Fine sea salt and freshly ground black pepper

Pinch of ground nutmeg

1 tablespoon finely chopped flat-leaf parsley

1 large clove garlic, crushed with the side of a large, heavy knife and finely chopped

¾ cup fresh breadcrumbs

2 tablespoons grated Parmigiano-Reggiano

1 tablespoon butter, melted

Place a large sauté pan over medium-low heat, and add the butter and olive oil. When the mixture foams, add the onion, and sauté, stirring occasionally, until very tender, about 10 minutes. Add the tomatoes, and cook, stirring, for 1 minute; then add the flour and stir to form a paste. Cook, stirring, for about 2 minutes, to eliminate the raw taste of the flour. Stir in the beef stock, and increase the heat to medium-high. When the mixture has just begun to simmer, add the diced beef, ½ teaspoon salt, several turns of the peppermill, and the nutmeg, parsley, and garlic. Cook, stirring occasionally, until the mixture has thickened, about 5 minutes.

Preheat the broiler to high. Transfer the beef and onion mixture to an 8- or 9-inch round or oval gratin dish, and smooth the top. In a small bowl, combine the breadcrumbs, Parmigiano, and melted butter; toss until the breadcrumbs are evenly moistened with butter. Scatter the breadcrumb mixture evenly over the beef, and broil until crisped and brown, about 4 minutes. Let stand for 3 minutes; then serve at once, with a green salad or sliced tomatoes.

LOBSTER CORN CAKES

— SERVES 2 TO 3 —

In this recipe, from Palm chef Jeffrey Bleaken of Philadelphia, you'll want to use clarified butter if you happen to have some languishing in the refrigerator from your last cooking effort (it keeps for months in a sealed container). However, since such a small quantity is called for, using whole butter is fine—it's not necessary to clarify a batch of butter just for a teaspoon or two. Here's the difference: whole butter contains milk solids, which will burn at a much lower temperature. So expect your lobster cakes to have a deep, golden-brown exterior, as opposed to the lighter gold crust that's produced with clarified butter. At the restaurant, Jeff likes to serve these with black bean salad.

1 pound cooked lobster meat, cut into
  ½-inch chunks
⅓ cup thawed frozen corn kernels, or
  cooked fresh corn
⅓ cup mayonnaise
1 tablespoon finely diced red bell pepper
1 tablespoon finely diced red onion
1 cup fresh white breadcrumbs
  (from about 2 slices)

1 to 2 teaspoons Worcestershire sauce,
  or to taste
Pinch of cayenne pepper
1 teaspoon Colman's mustard powder
1 large egg, lightly beaten
1 tablespoon butter, preferably clarified
Beurre Blanc, for serving (optional), or
  lemon wedges

In a large bowl, combine the lobster, corn, mayonnaise, red pepper, onion, breadcrumbs, Worcestershire sauce, cayenne, dry mustard, and beaten egg. Using a fork, mix lightly but thoroughly. Scoop up ½ cup of the mixture at a time, and use your hands to form patties, compressing to form a firm, dense cake. This mixture will make about 5 cakes. Place on a large plate, cover with plastic wrap, and refrigerate for 1 hour to firm the mixture.

Place a large nonstick skillet over medium-low heat, and add the butter. When the butter is hot, add the lobster cakes, and sauté on one side until golden brown. (Do not fry at too high a temperature, or the corn kernels may explode, or "pop.") Carefully turn, and sauté for 3 minutes more. Serve on warmed plates, drizzled with a little of the Beurre Blanc, or with a lemon wedge on the side

Beurre Blanc

YIELD: SCANT 1 CUP

3 tablespoons white wine vinegar

3 tablespoons dry white wine or vermouth

2½ tablespoons minced shallot

10 to 12 tablespoons cold unsalted butter, cut into ½-inch cubes

Fine sea salt and white pepper, preferably freshly ground

In a small saucepan, combine the vinegar, wine, and shallot. Place over medium heat, and bring to a simmer. Simmer until reduced to about 1½ teaspoons—just a loose glaze holding the shallots together. Cool the pan by tipping it to the side and carefully holding the base of the pan under cold running water for a few seconds. (At this point, you can set the reduction aside for up to 1 hour before finishing the sauce. Be sure to keep the butter cold and to reheat the reduction very gently before continuing.)

Away from the heat, whisk several cubes of the cold butter into the warm pan. Whisk until the butter no longer melts into the sauce. Then place the pan over low heat, and add several more cubes of cold butter, whisking just until the butter begins to melt. Occasionally, remove the pan from the heat if the mixture becomes too hot. (You need *some* heat to melt the butter, but if you leave the pan on the heat the fat will separate from the liquid and the sauce will be lost.) Repeat the process of adding cold butter and moving the pan on and off the heat as needed. The consistency of the finished sauce should be like that of heavy cream. You may not need all the butter—the sauce is finished when it has achieved a coating consistency. Add salt and pepper, and taste for seasoning, adjusting as necessary. If desired, strain the sauce through a small, fine-meshed sieve to remove the shallots, and drizzle over the plated lobster cakes.

CHAPTER 9

Desserts

Desserts, like many other dishes at the Palm, tend to be huge. For the unsuspecting diner, this can come as quite a surprise. But the desserts are really meant to be shared, which has become common practice among customers. People want the luscious, old-fashioned flavors of chocolate, sugar, fruit, and cream, but they don't want too much. Placing a big dessert in the center of the table and handing out forks all around also promotes a nice, familial feeling that diners seem to relish

Jeff Bleaken, chef at the Philadelphia Palm (and the widely acknowledged king of Palm desserts), enjoys making desserts because he really likes to eat them. "I like desserts that taste of something other than sugar," he says. "When they're oversweetened, the true flavor of the ingredients doesn't come through. To me, how a dessert tastes is far more important than what it looks like."

KEY LIME PIE

— SERVES 6 —

In certain parts of the country, key limes are easy to come by. In others, they show up in markets rarely, if at all. The Palm uses a bottled product called Nellie and Joe's Key Lime Juice, which is available in most good gourmet markets. See page 112 for tips on removing the flavorful zest from citrus fruits. The best tool for this process is a zester.

6 large egg yolks
1¾ cups (14 fluid ounces) sweetened
   condensed milk
⅔ cup fresh or bottled key lime juice
2 Persian (supermarket) limes, washed
   and dried

9-inch graham cracker crust (homemade or
   store-bought)
1 cup heavy cream, whipped to soft peaks
   with 1 teaspoon of sugar, for serving

Preheat the oven to 350°.

In a large bowl, combine the egg yolks, condensed milk, and key lime juice. Holding the whole limes over the bowl, use a zester to remove the zest, letting it fall into the mixture and reserving a little to use for garnish. Juice the zested limes, and add the juice to the bowl. Whisk the mixture thoroughly, and pour into the pie crust. Bake for 15 minutes. Cool to room temperature and refrigerate, covered with plastic wrap, for at least 4 and up to 48 hours. Cut into 6 wedges, and transfer to plates. Spoon a dollop of lightly sweetened whipped cream in the center of each slice, and scatter with a few shreds of the fresh lime zest. Serve at once.

NEW YORK CHEESECAKE

The Palm's cheesecake has been made by the same company (which shall remain nameless) since a Palm customer named Toby Beck brought in a cheesecake for Bruno Bozzi and Walter Ganzi (the fathers of the present owners, Bruce and Wally) back in 1965. It took the two partners one taste and approximately ten seconds to decide that this cheesecake would become the Palm's signature dessert, and it has been so ever since. "Dominic! Order this cheesecake!" cried Walter Ganzi Sr. "Forever!"

BROWNIE CHEESECAKE

— SERVES 10 TO 12 —

My favorite sweets — together! This luscious dessert is made in individual (3½ - inch) portions at the Palm, but I prefer the visual impact of this great, big, marbled creation. It slices beautifully, should be served warm with ice cream, and only has a few calories . . . when divided by 12. The recipe for this impressive centerpiece cake is from Jeffrey Bleaken of the Philadelphia Palm. Unlike most cheesecakes, this doesn't need to be refrigerated to set up. In fact, it's best when served right after the 1-hour cooling period.

BROWNIE LAYER:

1 cup (2 sticks) unsalted butter

1 cup Dutch-process cocoa powder

2 cups granulated sugar

4 large eggs

1 cup all-purpose flour

1 cup coarsely chopped walnuts

1 teaspoon best-quality vanilla extract

2 tablespoons fresh orange juice

CHEESECAKE LAYER:

2 pounds cream cheese, softened

1½ cups granulated sugar

4 large eggs

1 teaspoon best-quality vanilla extract

4 tablespoons Grand Marnier or Cointreau

Coffee or caramel ice cream, for serving

Lightly coat a 10-inch springform pan with vegetable oil spray. Preheat the oven to 325°, and place a rack in the center. In the top of a double boiler over medium heat, combine the butter and cocoa, stirring occasionally, until the butter is melted and the mixture is smooth. Stir in the sugar. Stir in the eggs, one at a time, until the mixture is smooth. Fold in the flour, walnuts, vanilla, and orange juice. Spread the brownie mixture evenly in the base of the prepared pan.

In a large bowl or an electric standing mixer, beat the cream cheese with the sugar at low speed until smooth. Add the eggs one at a time, beating well after each addition. Add the vanilla and Grand Marnier, and beat on high speed until fluffy, about 5 minutes more.

Spread the cheesecake mixture evenly over the brownie mixture, dragging a little of the brownie mixture upward in several places to create a marbled effect. Bake for 1 hour and 15 to 30 minutes, until puffed and golden, with just a slight tremble in the center. Remove from the oven, and run a knife around the edge of the cake to separate it from the pan. Cool in the pan on a rack for at least 1 hour; then transfer to a large platter, and remove the sides of the springform pan. Serve in wedges, with coffee or caramel ice cream.

"I used to be in public relations, and I discovered some pretty important stars, like Farrah Fawcett and Lee Majors. I had twenty-five clients—Sonny Bono, Burt Lancaster—and I got permission for all of them to go up on the wall at the Palm. But it took me twenty years more to have them put my own caricature up there. Now, I'm over the bar in West Hollywood."

—Jay Bernstein, Hollywood, California

CRÈME BRÛLÉE

— SERVES 10 —

"This is just about simple pleasure. The texture is what really makes a good crème brûlée—it should be like silk." —Jeffrey Bleaken, Philadelphia Palm chef

4 cups heavy cream
Grated zest of 1 lemon
8 large egg yolks
¾ cup superfine sugar
Pinch of fine sea salt

1 teaspoon best-quality vanilla extract
5 tablespoons superfine sugar, for the brûlée
About 30 raspberries
10 sprigs of fresh mint

Preheat the oven to 325°.

In a small saucepan, combine the cream and lemon zest, and place over high heat. Watch closely, and when bubbles appear around the edges and the liquid is about to boil, remove from the heat and let stand for 5 minutes.

In a large bowl, combine the egg yolks, sugar, and salt, and whisk until smooth. Whisking all the time, drizzle the hot cream into the yolk mixture in a thin stream. Whisk in the vanilla.

Strain the mixture through a fine sieve into ten 4-ounce ramekins, leaving a ¼-inch clearance at the top for the brûlée. Place the ramekins in a roasting pan large enough to hold them all without touching. Pour in boiling water to come about halfway up the sides of the ramekins, and loosely cover the pan with aluminum foil. Bake for 45 minutes to 1 hour, or until a quarter-sized circle in the center of each custard still trembles but is no longer liquid. Remove the ramekins from the water bath, and place on a baking sheet or tray. Let stand, uncovered, at room temperature for 2 hours (they will continue to cook and firm up slightly as they cool. Cover with plastic wrap, and refrigerate for at least 2 hours more, or overnight.

When ready to serve, scatter the top of each custard with 1½ teaspoons of superfine sugar, shaking gently to distribute the sugar layer as evenly as possible.

If you own a small kitchen blowtorch, use it to caramelize the sugar layer. The crème brûlée also may be caramelized under a home broiler, 3 at a time. Watch them closely, rotating frequently after the sugar starts bubbling to compensate for hot and cold spots. Garnish each ramekin with 3 raspberries and a sprig of mint, and serve immediately

In the years I spent writing this book, I attended a lot of Palm events. President and COO Fred Thimm is a fantastic speaker. He's motivational without being saccharine. The Palm's charity involvement is huge. Once it might have been P.R., but now, Fred says, it's time to give back. "It feels really good to be able to use our name and brand to help."

The whole idea of this privately held company is to become a big organization without becoming a "Big Organization." That Fred is the owner's son-in-law was forgotten long ago, about the time he moved from busboy to server back in 1981. Business school took him away for several years, and when he came back in 1990, there was never any question but that he would take on more and more responsibility. All of the modern-day business practices came with Fred. But ask other restaurateurs what they'd say about running at a 41 percent food cost, and watch their look of abject horror. Here, chefs get in trouble if it's lower—it's assumed they must be cutting corners!

PLUM-ALMOND CRISP

— SERVES 4 TO 5 —

Homey and exceedingly easy to make, this simple, colorful dessert benefits from really ripe plums (Philadelphia chef Jeffrey Bleaken prefers red plums) and the crisp, not-too-sweet texture of the topping.

FRUIT:

1¼ pounds plums, halved, pitted, and
   sliced ½ inch thick

2 large, ripe peaches, halved, pitted, and
   sliced ½ inch thick

¼ cup granulated sugar

1 tablespoon quick-cooking tapioca

½ teaspoon fresh lemon juice

Tiny pinch of fine sea salt

Butter, for preparing the pan

TOPPING:

¼ cup slivered, blanched almonds,
   finely chopped

¼ cup all-purpose flour

2 tablespoons light brown sugar

2 tablespoons granulated sugar

1½ teaspoons ground cinnamon

½ teaspoon ground nutmeg
Pinch of ground cardamom
¼ cup unsalted butter, melted

⅓ cup quick-cooking oatmeal
Vanilla ice cream, for serving (optional)

In a large bowl, combine the plums, peaches, sugar, tapioca, lemon juice, and salt. Toss to combine, and let stand for 30 minutes, to allow the fruit to exude its juices. Butter a 6 x 12-inch baking pan.

Preheat the oven to 350°.

In another bowl, combine the almonds, flour, brown and white sugars, cinnamon, nutmeg, cardamom, butter, and oatmeal. Toss together until evenly blended.

Spoon the fruit into the prepared pan. Cover evenly with the topping, pressing it down slightly to help it adhere. Bake for about 45 minutes, until the topping is golden brown. Cool on a rack for 15 minutes; then use a large spoon to serve, accompanied by vanilla ice cream, if desired.

APPLE-CRANBERRY CRUMBLE PIE

— SERVES 6 —

"This was a seasonal item that just wouldn't die. The customers wouldn't let me take it off the menu. There are times when you can't get fresh or frozen cranberries, but you could try using dried cranberries. Just soak them in warm water for 30 minutes to plump them up." —Jeff Bleaken, Philadelphia Palm chef

TOPPING:
⅔ cup all-purpose flour
¼ cup light brown sugar
2 tablespoons granulated sugar
¼ teaspoon ground cinnamon

½ cup halved pecans, finely chopped
¼ cup quick-cooking oatmeal
5 tablespoons unsalted butter, melted
¼ teaspoon best-quality vanilla extract

FRUIT:
¾ cup light brown sugar
¼ cup granulated sugar
⅓ cup all-purpose flour
¾ pound Granny Smith or other cooking
   apples, peeled, cored, and thickly sliced

2 cups fresh or thawed frozen cranberries
1 teaspoon ground cinnamon
3 tablespoons unsalted butter, cut into
   ¼-inch dice

¾ pound Golden Delicious apples, peeled,
  cored, and thickly sliced

10-inch unbaked pie shell (homemade or
  store-bought)

Vanilla ice cream, for serving (optional)

In a large bowl, combine all the ingredients for the topping, and toss together until evenly blended.

Preheat the oven to 400°. In another large bowl, combine the brown sugar, granulated sugar, flour, apples, cranberries, cinnamon, and butter. Toss together until thoroughly blended.

Spoon the apple mixture into the pie shell, pressing slightly to make sure it all fits securely (it will be quite tall). Scatter the topping evenly over the top of the pie, pressing it gently into any gaps in the fruit layer to help it adhere. Place on a baking sheet, and bake for about 45 minutes, until the fruit is tender and the topping is golden brown. Keep an eye on the pie as it's baking; if the topping seems to be browning too quickly, tent it loosely with aluminum foil. Cool on a rack for 15 minutes, and serve warm, cut into wedges, accompanied by a scoop of vanilla ice cream, if desired.

SUMMER PUDDING

— SERVES 4, CAN BE DOUBLED —

If some of the berries listed below are unavailable, just increase the quantities of any berries you can find to compensate. If any less common varieties of berries turn up in your market or garden, add them to the mixture as well. It stands to reason that, even in this age of air-lifted fruits, this fabulous English dessert is best saved for the summer months.

1 pint strawberries, hulled and halved, or
  quartered if large
¾ cup granulated sugar
1 pint blueberries
1½ pints raspberries
½ pint blackberries

Pinch of fine sea salt
Fresh lemon juice, if necessary
12 slices white bread, from a sandwich-style
  loaf
1 cup whipping cream, whipped to soft peaks
  (optional)

THE PALM RESTAURANT COOKBOOK

In a large, nonreactive saucepan, combine the strawberries and the sugar. Stir over medium heat for about 5 minutes, just until the juices begin to run and the sugar has dissolved. Add the remaining berries, and stir to combine. Cook gently for 6 to 8 minutes more, until the berries have released a good deal of juice. Stir in the salt and taste for sweetness, adding a few drops of lemon juice if the mixture is too sweet, or a pinch more sugar if it is too tart.

Line four 8-ounce ramekins with plastic wrap, pressing it into the corners and around the sides. Using one of the ramekins as a guide, use a small, sharp knife to cut 12 rounds from the bread slices. Using a slotted spoon so that all the juices remain in the saucepan, transfer about 2 tablespoons of the berry mixture into each ramekin. Dip both sides of a bread round into the berry juices, and place on top of the berries. Continue dipping and layering bread and berries until you have used all the berries, ending with a final bread round. If any juice is left over, drizzle it around the edges. Don't worry if the bread rises a little higher than the rims of the ramekins. Cover each ramekin with a sheet of plastic wrap, and weight it with a small saucer that fits just inside the rim of the ramekin. Press each saucer down slightly to compress the bread by about ¾ inch. Then place one ramekin on top of another, and refrigerate the two stacks for at least 4 hours, or overnight.

When ready to serve, remove the saucers and top sheets of plastic wrap, and fold back the lower sheets of plastic. Invert each pudding onto a dessert plate, and peel off the remaining plastic wrap. Serve at once, with a dollop of whipped cream, if desired.

Chocolate Ganache Cake

— SERVES 12 —

This cake batter is incredibly forgiving. If you have a fear of making baked desserts, this is the cake for you. The batter almost makes itself, and you can practically play catch with the finished cake—it won't crumble. Yet the texture is rich and moist, a perfect foil for the luscious ganache. In reality, of course, the cake is really just a vehicle for the ganache, so don't hesitate to splurge on a really good chocolate, such as Valrhona.

GANACHE:

1 pound best-quality semisweet chocolate, coarsely chopped (or use chocolate chips)

2 cups whipping cream

CAKE:

Softened butter and all-purpose flour, for preparing the pan

¾ cup Dutch-process cocoa powder

1¾ cups all-purpose flour

2 cups granulated sugar

½ tablespoon baking powder

1 teaspoon fine sea salt

½ tablespoon baking soda

½ cup canola or other flavorless vegetable oil

3 large eggs, lightly beaten

1 cup whole milk

1 cup boiling water

Confectioners sugar, for dusting the finished cake

To make the ganache: Combine the chocolate and cream in the top of a double boiler, and place over low heat. Stir occasionally, and when most of the chocolate has melted, remove the pan from the heat, stirring every few minutes until all the chocolate has melted and the mixture is thick and smooth. Transfer the ganache to a metal mixing bowl, and allow it to come to room temperature. Refrigerate, stirring thoroughly every 20 minutes, until the ganache reaches a spreadable consistency, like that of peanut butter. This will take 1½ to 2 hours and may be done the night before, if desired. Once the ganache is thickened, there is no need to continue stirring it. Use while it is still spreadable, as further refrigeration will make it too firm to spread.

To make the cake: Preheat the oven to 350°. Generously butter a 10- x 3-inch round cake pan. Cut a round of parchment paper to fit in the base of the pan, using the pan as a guide. Fit the parchment round into the pan, and butter it. Add about ⅓ cup flour to the pan, shake it to coat all sides evenly, and then tap out the excess. If the pan has a removable bottom, wrap the base tightly with aluminum foil to prevent the uncooked batter from seeping out. Place the prepared pan on a baking sheet.

Sift the cocoa powder, flour, sugar, baking powder, salt, and baking soda into the bowl of an electric standing mixer. Mix on slow speed for 1 minute; then turn off the machine, and add the oil, eggs, and milk. Mix on medium speed for 2 minutes; then stop the mixer to scrape down the sides of the bowl. Add the boiling water, and mix for 1 minute more. The batter will be very thin. Pour the batter into the prepared pan, and place in the center of the oven. Bake for 45 minutes, until the cake begins to shrink away from the sides of the pan. Cool on a rack to room temperature; then run a small knife around the edge of the cake to release the sides, and turn out onto a work surface. Slice the cake horizontally into three 1-inch layers, using a long, serrated bread knife and placing your hand atop the cake to help guide the knife evenly. Turn the cake several times to be sure you are cutting even layers. (Take care that the cake is completely cool before you frost it, or the ganache will melt on contact with the warm cake.) Spread half the ganache evenly on the bottom cake layer; then top it with the middle layer, matching up the edges. Spread this layer with the remaining ganache; then cover with the third cake round, with the parchment side on top. Peel off the parchment. Refrigerate the cake for at least 1 hour, and up to 24 hours, to firm the ganache. Allow to return to room temperature before serving, for the best flavor. Dust generously with confectioners sugar, and cut into wedges.

TIRAMISU

"This dish must be refrigerated for twenty-four hours; otherwise it won't set up and won't slice nicely. Me and a young kitchen worker named Caesar, in L.A., worked on this forever to get it right, and I hate to say this because it sounds conceited, but I have never had a better one. And I've eaten at a lot of Italian restaurants. People eat our tiramisu and say, 'I can't f***'in believe it.' They've never had such a great tiramisu, either." —Tony Tammero, executive chef

1 cup heavy cream
4 large egg yolks (see Note)
1 tablespoon Meyer's or other dark rum,
　Amaretto, Kahlua, or Godiva liqueur
1 scant tablespoon Hershey's or other
　chocolate syrup

⅓ cup superfine sugar
1⅔ cups mascarpone, softened at room
　temperature for 1 hour
3 (3½-ounce) packages ladyfinger cookies
3 cups very strong, cold coffee
Cocoa powder, for dusting

In a large, cold bowl, whip the cream to stiff peaks. Refrigerate until ready to assemble the tiramisu.

In the bowl of an electric standing mixer, combine the egg yolks, rum, chocolate syrup, and sugar. Beat the mixture at high speed for 2 minutes. It should be quite thick and leave a trail when the beater is lifted away. Place the softened mascarpone in a large mixing bowl, and gently fold in the beaten egg-and-chocolate mixture. Fold in the chilled whipped cream.

Dip each ladyfinger briefly into the coffee, and arrange in rows on the bottom of a rectangular (preferably 6- x 12-inch) baking dish. Gently spread an even layer of the mascarpone mixture over the ladyfingers, and top with a second layer of coffee-dipped ladyfingers. Spread with the mascarpone mixture, make a third layer of ladyfingers, and end with a layer of the mascarpone. Cover the pan tightly with plastic wrap, and refrigerate for no less than 24 hours, and up to 36 hours. Cut into squares for serving, and dust each one generously with cocoa powder.

Note: This dish contains raw egg yolks. The elderly, the very young, pregnant women, and those with compromised immune systems may wish to avoid consuming raw egg yolks if salmonella is a problem in your area.

Rice Pudding with Rum-Soaked Raisins

— Serves 4 Palm-Style, or 6 —

This is like really yummy baby food, enhanced with a little rum for grown-ups who still, on tough days, want to feel like somebody's baby. For 1 cup of cooked rice, bring a small saucepan of water to a rapid boil and add a tiny pinch of salt. Add ⅓ cup long-grain white rice, and boil, uncovered, for 20 minutes. Drain in a sieve.

½ cup raisins
⅓ cup Meyer's or other dark rum
½ teaspoon best-quality vanilla extract
2¾ cups whole milk
1 cup cooked white rice (leftover is fine)
⅓ cup plus 1 tablespoon granulated sugar

½ tablespoons unsalted butter
⅛ teaspoon fine sea salt
6 large eggs
½ cup heavy cream
Ground cinnamon, for serving
Fresh berries, for serving (optional)

In a small bowl, combine the raisins, rum, and vanilla. Toss together and set aside.

In a large, heavy saucepan, combine the milk, rice, sugar, butter, and salt. Place over medium heat, and stir until the sugar has dissolved, about 2 minutes. Reduce the heat so the liquid simmers gently. Partially cover the pan, and simmer for 40 minutes, stirring occasionally, until thick and soupy.

In a bowl, whisk together the eggs and cream until smooth. Whisk a quarter of the hot rice mixture briskly into the egg-and-cream mixture; then return this combination to the rice pan. Keep the pan over medium-low heat, and stir constantly until thickened, only about 2 minutes. Do not allow the mixture to boil, or the eggs will scramble! Stir in the raisins, along with any juices remaining in the bowl. Ladle the mixture into four 12-ounce ramekins or a 1½-quart soufflé dish, and place a piece of plastic wrap directly onto the top surface of the pudding (to prevent a skin from forming). Refrigerate for at least 3, and up to 24, hours. Remove from the refrigerator about 10 minutes before serving, and carefully peel away the plastic wrap. Sprinkle with a little cinnamon and some fresh berries, if desired.

CARROT CAKE

"My sous-chef, Ritchie, came up with this recipe. At the time, his frosting was a little gritty. I don't know why, but then he figured out that using superfine sugar and beating the cream cheese and butter until they are nice and fluffy makes a perfect icing, with no grit." —Jeffrey Bleaken, Philadelphia Palm chef

CAKE:

3 cups all-purpose flour

2 cups granulated sugar

½ tablespoon baking soda

1 tablespoon baking powder

2 teaspoons ground cinnamon

½ teaspoon ground nutmeg

½ teaspoon fine sea salt

1½ cups canola or other vegetable oil

5 large eggs

1½ teaspoons best-quality vanilla extract

1½ pounds carrots, grated (4½ cups)

¾ cup raisins

¾ cup pecan pieces

Butter and all-purpose flour, for preparing the pan

FROSTING:

1½ pound cream cheese, softened

4 ounces unsalted butter, softened

1 cup superfine sugar

Zest of one orange, finely grated

Confectioners sugar, for dusting

Preheat the oven to 350°.

In the bowl of an electric standing mixer, combine the flour, sugar, baking soda, baking powder, cinnamon, nutmeg, and salt. Mix on slow speed to combine. In a large measuring cup, whisk together the oil, eggs, and vanilla. Pour the egg mixture into the dry ingredients, and add the carrots. Mix on the slowest speed until evenly blended. The batter will be very thick. Fold in the raisins and pecans.

Butter and flour a 10-inch round cake pan with 3-inch sides. Scoop the batter into the prepared pan, and smooth the top. Bake for 65 to 70 minutes, or until the sides begin to shrink away from the pan and a toothpick inserted into the center of the cake comes out clean. Cool on a rack to room temperature.

While the cake is baking, make the frosting. In a large bowl, beat the cream cheese, butter, and superfine sugar vigorously with a wooden spoon until fluffy. Stir in the orange zest.

Run a small knife around the edge of the cake pan to release the sides, and turn out onto a work surface. Slice the cake horizontally into three 1-inch layers, using a long, serrated bread knife and placing your hand atop the cake to help guide the knife evenly. Turn the cake several times to be sure you are cutting even layers. (Take care that the cake is completely cool before you frost it, or the warmth of the cake will melt the frosting on contact.) Spread one cake layer with about a quarter of the frosting; then top it with the second cake layer, matching up the edges. Spread with another quarter of the frosting. Cover with the third cake round, and frost the top and sides of the cake evenly with the remaining frosting. Refrigerate for at least 1 hour, and up to 24 hours, to firm the frosting. For the best flavor, allow to return to room temperature before serving. Dust generously with confectioners sugar, and cut into wedges.

JEFFREY'S ZABAGLIONE

— SERVES 6 —

Jeff Bleaken makes this on the fly, almost without thinking, whenever he has nice fresh strawberries. One of the classic flavors of Italian cuisine, it is also fabulous over fresh figs, preferably still warm from the summer sun shining on the tree. Jeff prepares this directly over the burner, but the temperature is so crucial, because of the danger of curdling the egg yolks, that it's far safer to make it in a double boiler over barely simmering water. Be aware that this mixture almost quadruples in volume! If you don't have a really large top for your double boiler, substitute a large metal mixing bowl set over a saucepan of water.

4 large egg yolks
¼ cup granulated sugar

⅓ cup marsala, preferably Florio

Place the egg yolks and the sugar in the top of a double boiler, off the heat; whisk, using a balloon whisk or an electric beater, until the mixture is pale yellow and creamy. Place the top of the double boiler over a pan on the stove containing about 1 inch of barely simmering water (make sure the water does not touch the base of the double boiler). Add the marsala, and continue to whisk or beat, without stopping, for about 10 minutes, until the mixture begins to foam and then swells into a soft, frothy mass. Serve warm, in large spoonfuls, over fresh berries or other ripe fruit.

INDEX

Bold page numbers refer to photographs.

Eggs, in straciatella Romano, 45
Escarole, in straciatella Romano, 45

F

Filet mignon. *See under* Beef
Fish, 70
    anchovies: in Monday night salad, 52; in roasted red
peppers and, 56, **132**
        red snapper Capri, 75
        salmon: blackened, 77; horseradish-crusted, 79
        sole meuniere, Dover, 79
        swordfish steak with citrus butter, broiled, 76
        tuna: with field greens and soy vinaigrette,
            sesame-seared ahi, 38; with red wine and
            shallot demiglace, rosemary-seared, 81
Fontina, filet mignon sandwich with roasted peppers,
fried eggplant, and, **131,** 182
French-fried onions, **130,** 173
Fruit
    apple-cranberry crumble pie, 195
    berries, in summer pudding, **136,** 196
    citrus butter, for broiled swordfish steak, 77
    lemons, 112; in chicken citron, 115
    mango salsa, 73, **128**
    pineapple, in mango salsa, 73, **128**
    plum-almond crisp, 194
    raisins, rum-soaked, rice pudding with, 200
    tangerines, in California steak salad with red onions,
        watercress, tangerines, and black pepper
        vinaigrette, 177

G

Garlic and oil. *See* Aglio e olio
Gigi salad, 51
Goat cheese, rigatoni with portobello mushrooms and,
    151
Gorgonzola, arugula, and radicchio, grilled beefsteak
    salad with, 60
Green beans. *See under* Vegetable dishes
Green peppercorns, in steak au poivre, 94
Greens. *See* Salads
Grilled dishes
    beefsteak salad with Gorgonzola, arugula, and
        radicchio, 60
    chicken: Caesar salad, 57; and roasted red pepper
        sandwich, 138
    chopped steak, 99
    jumbo shrimp over baby field greens, 36
    prime aged porterhouse, 88

H

Half and half, **130,** 168
Ham
    in chef salad, 56
    hocks, in split pea soup, 48
    prosciutto, in chicken Medici, 137
Hash, roast beef, 183
Hash browns, 166
Hearts of lettuce with blue cheese dressing, 64
Hearts of palm salad, 41
Hors d'oeuvres. *See* Appetizers
Horseradish-crusted salmon, 79
Hot dogs, Tony's superb, 101

J

Jeff Phillips' hot blueberry tea, 27
Jeffrey's blackening spice, 78
    dishes using, 59, 74, 77, 114
Jeffrey's famous dressing, 67
Jeffrey's zabaglione, 202

K

Key lime pie, 190
Knockwurst, lentil soup with, 47

L

Lamb chops
    double-cut Maryland, 95, **122**
    with rosemary, 96
Lasagna, Tony's mom's, 155
Leaf spinach, 161
Leftovers, dishes using. *See also* Beef
    filet mignon: grilled, salad with Gorgonzola, arugula,
        and radicchio, 60; sandwich with roasted
        peppers, fried eggplant, and fontina, **131,** 182
    lobster corn cakes, 186
    roast beef hash, 183
    steak: and braised onions under a Parmesan crust, 185;
        California salad with red onions, watercress,
        tangerines, and black pepper vinaigrette, 177;
        cold sliced, with salsa verde, 181; salad with
        "au jus" dressing, tomatoes, and romaine, 176;
        salad with butter lettuce, Gruyere croûtes, and
        Niçoise olives, 178; Thai salad with basil and
        mint, 179
    uptown chile con carne, 184
Lentil soup with knockwurst, 47
Lettuce, hearts of, with blue cheese dressing, 64
Linguine. *See under* Pasta

Rice
    pudding with rum-soaked raisins, 200
    risotto Milanese, 153
Rigatoni with portobello mushrooms and goat cheese, 151
Risotto Milanese, 153
Roast beef
    hash, 183
    prime rib, 90, **125**
    in steak and braised onions under a Parmesan crust, 185
    in uptown chile con carne, 184
Roasted red peppers. *See under* Peppers, sweet red
Rosemary-seared tuna with red wine and shallot
        demiglace, 81

S

Salad dressings
    balsamic, 68; salads using: chopped tomato and onion,
        61; green bean and onion, 63; hearts of palm,
        41; roasted red peppers and anchovies, 56, **132**
    blue cheese, 64; salads using: chopped tomato and
        onion, 61; green bean and onion, 63; hearts of
        lettuce, 64; hearts of palm, 41; roasted red
        peppers and anchovies, 56, **132**
    Caesar, 65; for grilled chicken Caesar salad, 57
    Jeffrey's famous, 67; salads using: chopped tomato and
        onion, 61; green bean and onion, 63; hearts of
        palm, 41; roasted red peppers and anchovies,
        56, **132**
    ranch, 66; for blackened filet spinach salad, 59
    roasted red pepper, 67; salads using: chopped tomato
        and onion, 61; green bean and onion, 63; hearts
        of palm, 41; roasted red peppers and anchovies,
        56
    vinaigrette, basic, 65; salads using: chef, 57; chopped
        tomato and onion, 61; Cobb-Stein, 55; Gigi, 51;
        green bean and onion, 63; hearts of palm, 41;
        Monday night salad, 52; roasted red peppers and
        anchovies, 56, **132**; west side cobb, 53
    vinaigrette, black pepper, 177
    vinaigrette, soy, 38
Salads
    beef: with "au jus" dressing, tomatoes, and romaine,
        176; blackened filet spinach salad, 59; with
        butter lettuce, Gruyere croûtes, and Niçoise
        olives, 178; California, with red onions,
        watercress, tangerines, and black pepper
        vinaigrette, 177; in chef salad, 56; grilled, with
        Gorgonzola, arugula, and radicchio, 60; Thai,
        with basil and mint, 179

chicken: in chef salad, 56; grilled Caesar, 57; west
        side cobb, 53
    fish: anchovies, in Monday night salad, 52; roasted red
        peppers and anchovies, 56, **132**; sesame-seared
        ahi tuna with field greens and soy vinaigrette, 38
    ham, in chef salad, 56
    shellfish: grilled jumbo shrimp over baby field greens,
        36; lobster cobb wrap, 54; shrimp, in Gigi, 51
    turkey, in Cobb-Stein, 55
    vegetables: arugula, for veal malfata, 110, **127**; buffalo
        mozzarella with tomatoes, basil, and virgin olive
        oil, 62; chopped tomato and onion, 61; green
        bean and onion, 63; hearts of lettuce with blue
        cheese dressing, 64; hearts of palm, 41
Salmon
    blackened, 77
    horseradish-crusted, 79
Salsa
    mango, 73, **128**
    verde, cold sliced steak with, 181
Sandwiches
    filet mignon, with roasted peppers, fried eggplant,
        and fontina, **131,** 182
    grilled chicken and roasted red pepper, 138
    lobster cobb wrap, 54
Sauces and condiments
    Bearnaise, 92
    Bolognese, 154
    citrus butter, 77
    clam: red, 143; white, **124,** 142
    curry, 118
    for lasagna, Tony's mom's, 155
    mango salsa, 73, **128**
    marinara, 146; recipes using: spaghetti marinara, 146;
        string beans, **130,** 164; veal parmigiana, 104
    onion, New York hot red, 102
    pesto, 139
    salsa verde, 181
Sausages
    Italian, in Tony's mom's lasagna, 155
    knockwurst, lentil soup with, 47
    mortadella and arugula à la Tony, linguine with, **123,**
        144
Seafood. *See* Fish; Shellfish
Sesame-seared ahi tuna with field greens and soy
        vinaigrette, 38
Shellfish, 70. *See also* Fish
    calamari fritti, 37
    clam(s), 30; bianco, 32, **135**; casino, 30, **135**;